THE
POWER
OF
A FEW
KIND WORDS

THE
POWER
OF
A FEW
KIND WORDS

CREATE A MORE MEANINGFUL LIFE,
ONE LETTER AT A TIME

———

Tracey Willis Gates

Epigraph Books
Rhinebeck, New York

Hardcover ISBN 978-1-960090-37-9
Paperback ISBN 978-1-960090-38-6
eBook ISBN 978-1-960090-39-3

Library of Congress Control Number 2023918077

Book and cover design by Colin Rolfe

Epigraph Books
22 East Market Street, Suite 304
Rhinebeck, New York 12572
(845) 876-4861
epigraphps.com

———

To Tom, my advocate, my fixer, my everything.
To Ren, Jenna, Sheridan, Colin, Hudson, and
Maverick who truly light up my world.
To my mother, Janet Willis, for her belief in me, and
to my father, Buzz Willis, for his unconditional love.

Contents

A Note to the Reader

What kind of person do you want to be?

Kindness can be simple. And yet it has the power to change the world, one person at a time. If all of humankind led with kindness, I believe there would be more collaboration, respect, productivity, joy, calm, and mindful living in this messy, dysfunctional, beautiful world we share.

So, as you read this book, please ask yourself, "What *kind* of person do I want to be?"

Introduction

"Every action you take is a vote for the type of person you wish to become. No single instance will transform your beliefs, but as the votes build up, so does the evidence of your new identity."

—James Clear, author of *Atomic Habits*

I KNOCKED ON the red door of the cream-colored house diagonally across the street from mine. I carried a bouquet of sunflowers in one hand and a card in the other. When Mary opened the door, I wasn't sure she recognized me. I introduced myself and apologized that it had taken me twenty-two years and ten months to cross the street and officially meet our neighbors.

For over two decades I'd watched Mary and Joe, who I think are now in their eighties, walk around the neighborhood holding hands. They looked perfectly paired, both slight in stature, his goatee matching the color of her pixie haircut. Each time I saw them, hand-in-hand, on their comfortable lockstep stroll, I would smile, pause, and admire them from afar. Their partnership was evident, and it made me hopeful that my husband and I may be walking together like them in our later years.

Although we waved while getting the mail or driving by, we had never officially met. There was no good reason for this oversight. It just never happened. However, I'd been having kind thoughts about Mary and Joe for all those years, it was time that they knew it. I handed the flowers and card to Mary and told her how much I appreciated watching them hold hands over the years. I told her they were silent role models for me for how a companionable partnership should be.

Mary looked down at her feet like a shy young girl. When she lifted her head, her eyes were glistening. She told me how touched she was that I came over and shared those words with her. Then she reached her slender arms up and gave me a hug. Everything I said, I had written in the card that I asked her to share with Joe. And as I headed back across the street, I was filled with that warm feeling you get when you know you've made a meaningful connection. I was smiling from the inside out.

A few days later, in the mail, I received a lovely card from Mary and Joe thanking me for the gesture of friendship. So let me tell you from firsthand experience: **It's never too late to share our kind thoughts, even if they're decades overdue. Sharing those thoughts simply feels good to both the writer and the recipient.**

* * *

If sharing our kind thoughts feels somewhere on the spectrum between good and spectacular for both the giver and receiver, requires no special degree or talent, and just takes a little effort, then why is it so often absent from our to-do list?

We fill our days with things that make us feel good. We're quite good at this. We can eat an entire pint of Peanut Paradise ice cream in one sitting. We can binge-watch an entire series on Netflix over the course of a weekend. But we so often don't take the time to share our kind thoughts, which always feels good.

Kindness is universally acknowledged to be a valued and sought-after trait, so much so that it has its own international holiday. November 13th is World Kindness Day. Yet, why do we rarely make it a priority?

I've spent the last few years grappling with this question. I went on an odyssey to see what would happen if I binged kindness the way I binge other things that make me feel good. I put kindness, through writing unexpected letters of appreciation, on my daily to-do list for one year. What I learned is that kindness takes practice and intention but is deeply gratifying in a way that makes life sweeter than any ice cream. So this is my story. I hope it may motivate you to put down your spoon, turn off the remote for a few minutes, and try sharing your own kind thoughts when you have them.

* * *

Connections nourish me—and I believe they will do the same for you. We feel more alive and more vital after meaningful conversation, both with people we know well and those we don't. We are lifted up and energized when we can share, listen, support, and laugh with our fellow humans.

When I became a life and wellness coach many years ago, I felt like I had come home. My passion for authentic connections and my purpose to let people everywhere know they matter are now intertwined in a way that fuels my soul. One of the most powerful exercises I encourage my clients to do is write an unexpected letter of appreciation. This isn't a thank you letter but what I call a "just because" letter. It's a way to feel good about yourself and at the same time, help someone feel good about themselves. For many people, this can mean stepping out of their comfort zone and being willing to get a bit vulnerable.

I choose to believe we all have kind thoughts about people, but for reasons that elude me, we so often neglect to share them. When we do, beautiful connections happen. The most surprising connection is with ourselves. We tend to like who we are when we share appreciations. When we become mindfully present and fill ourselves with positive thoughts about another person, the energizing, empowering, and uplifting feelings linger.

* * *

I had always enjoyed writing letters of appreciation, but then one day I realized I wasn't making it a priority anymore. I was allowing life to get in the way of connection.

My glass-half-full attitude began to dip close to the half-empty midline allowing a mist of negativity to insidiously settle into my mind, body, and daily life. In addition to the nightly news and the unbearable national political discourse, my sister Wendy and I were caring for our aging, courageous, and fiercely independent mother. After agonizing debate, we all agreed to move Mom into a continuing care retirement community (CCRC).

Wendy and I were forced into a role we never wanted. We became expert advocates for Mom as we endlessly navigated her care and multiple moves throughout the new facility. She had to give up her independent living apartment, which we had painstakingly decorated to reflect her prior home, when she broke her hip after sleeping there just forty-two nights. She then had three months and ten days in skilled nursing, thirteen months in assisted living, and then back to skilled nursing for the last two months of her life. Sprinkled throughout this period were eight hospital visits, and finally, three days in hospice.

The month we moved Mom into her CCRC, I developed an autoimmune disease called polymyalgia rheumatica (PMR), which caused debilitating pain in my arms and legs. I feel certain this was stress induced. I take my health seriously. I try to eat well and exercise. But although I taught my clients about the harmful effects of the stress-induced cortisol rollercoaster, I neglected to pay attention to it myself until I needed my husband, Tom, to help me get dressed and stand up.

This difficult time caused me to do some deep reflection. If constant worry and anxiety can cause the body to break down, could intentional doses of kindness and mindfulness repair the body, mind, and soul?

I decided to conduct an experiment. I wanted to see if I could feel calmer, more connected, happier, and have less physical pain if I shared my kind thoughts with intention. I wanted to fill all the little spaces in my being with kindness, compassion, and love. I wanted to do a cleanse. Not the kind that involves drinking horrible things and eating no sugar, but the kind that purges negative thinking and makes room for the light of positivity to get in through the cracks. This was a negativity cleanse.

I challenged myself to write a handwritten, unexpected letter of appreciation to a different person every day for one year. This forced me to slow down and engage in a way I had been neglecting while I was retreating into myself and my worries.

I began to realize there were opportunities for connection everywhere. I proactively started to look for the positive attributes, both big and small, each one of us possesses. Then, I wrote my appreciations down and mailed them the old-fashioned way... yes, with a stamp, and yes, I was able to find people's addresses.

The letters were always a surprise and never sent around a holiday or birthday. The unexpectedness, I found, added another layer of delight. I wrote them on 4"-by-6" folded notecards, usually filling the top and the bottom of the card with my kind thoughts. The notes were not long but always authentic. I was doing my small part to make the world feel a little more love, and in doing so, fill my soul with the kindness and gentleness it craved.

This project I initiated to make me feel better had a ripple effect I never could have imagined. The recipients of my letters called, wrote, emailed, texted, and told me in person how my letter made their day, brought them to tears, or filled them with positive energy. It's called intentional kindness, and it's a superpower that's available to all of us.

This experiment to see if I could positively influence my emotional and physical wellbeing through writing unexpected letters of appreciation shocked my system back into a regular rhythm and transformed my life. Within a few weeks, I was noticing changes.

I felt better about myself. I was less anxious about my mother's care and better equipped to handle the daily challenges. I was feeling more present and less alone as I took time to connect with people in a more deliberate way. My physical symptoms were subsiding along with my stress. As the weeks and months went by, I was calmer, more connected, and happier.

What became apparent is that negativity creates an unwanted tension and positivity creates a welcomed tolerance. My experiment was quite simply a joyful journey that reminded me we're all more powerful than we might think.

Learning New Habits

Sometimes we hang on to a certain way of living simply because we don't know a better way. This book offers you a healthier way to approach your interactions which I believe can lead you to more abundant living.

An eighty-five year study on what makes a person happy over a lifetime has reinforced my personal research. The directors of the multigeneration Harvard Study of Adult Development, Dr. Robert Waldinger and Dr. Marc Schulz, write in *The Good Life: Lessons from the World's Longest Scientific Study of Happiness*, "we underestimate the beneficial effects of human connection." Dr. Waldinger maintains, "if you're going to do one thing this year to ensure your own health and happiness, find the time to nurture and develop relationships. That's what makes for a meaningful life."

This surprising research found that the happiest people were also the healthiest because "relationships get into our bodies and shape our health. Good relationships are stress regulators. Taking care of your body is important but tending to your relationships is a form of self-care too." Waldinger and Schulz define the process of caring for our relationships as "social fitness." "It's just as crucial as physical fitness," explains Waldinger, who added that "neglected relationships can atrophy, like muscles. Our social life is a living system, and it needs exercise."[1] Luckily for us, it's never too late to incorporate this form of fitness into our daily routines, regardless of age.

Imagine a world filled with people who prioritize their "social fitness." I want to encourage you to put this type of intentional kindness on your to-do list. No missed opportunities for connection.

If you want to feel calmer, more connected, and happier, avoid playing the "I'm too busy" card. We all have a few minutes to think positive thoughts and then release them when we decide to make it a priority. When you send appreciations out into the world, unsolicited, it feels delicious. Squeeze it in between doing the laundry and making that dreaded phone call to Verizon. I guarantee you'll be more patient on that call. Or take a few minutes to share with your colleague what you appreciate about them and experience a positive shift in collaboration. Leave a letter on your teenager's pillow and tell them why you think they're so fabulous. They need to hear it, and it will be a powerful reminder for you of their precious gifts.

What was reinforced for me 365 times, and many more since, is that when we release our kind thoughts and share them, we nourish ourselves. This is an important part of our mental hygiene. As this practice made me happier, it also cleared the way for more focus, more confidence, and more peace. But don't take my word for it. This practice is available to you. No degree or certification of any kind required. All you need is a pen, paper, maybe stamps, and the willingness to be a little vulnerable.

I'm so excited for you to try it. You don't have to write a letter a day for a year. Just try it once and see how it feels. If you like it, try it again the next time you have a kind thought about someone.

Kindness is learned behavior. You're not born kind or unkind. You just have to practice it. Mr. Fitzpatrick, our children's elementary school principal, always said, "Practice makes improvement." That's why I call it an intentional kindness practice because you have to keep working at it.

Kindness can be difficult. It can mean making the hard choice over an easy one. It can take time and energy we don't think we have. Houston Kraft, author of *Deep Kindness* and co-founder of Character Strong, says "Nice happens because we have the time. Kind happens because we make the time."[2]

What I heard over and over during my year of intentional kindness was "No one has ever done this for me before." Why is it so hard for us to share our kind thoughts? It shatters me to think that people may go through their whole life never being told how awesome they are. Together we can make sharing our kind thoughts a common practice. The letter you send becomes a tangible keepsake that captures your gratitude in a permanent way for someone to savor for years to come. It's hard to throw away kind and loving thoughts about yourself.

Don't Let Fear Get in the Way

When was the last time you received or wrote an unexpected letter of appreciation? Does the idea of writing a letter like this make you concerned how the letter will be received?

Are you worried you'll be seen as wanting something, or even that your penmanship or grammar will be judged? Maybe the thought of getting a little vulnerable makes you shy away from this, or you just don't have the time?

As you read about my journey, I hope these possible objections will be lessened. Research by Stephen Toefler and his team at Kent State University has shown that when we express our gratitude through letters of appreciation, life satisfaction goes up, happiness goes up, and depression goes down—all outcomes I can attest to.[3]

One thing we can change in this uncertain world is how we treat each other. In this book, I'll provide you with motivation and practical tips to help you make room for this intentional kindness practice in your life. I'll introduce you to my adored father who was the inspiration for this book. I explain why his mantra of only wanting "a few kind words" has become my mantra and the title of this book. I share what he meant to me as a child, his untimely passing, and the power and the closure I felt when I finally read aloud *a few kind words* to him 33 years after he died. I also share touching stories of connection that happened over my yearlong journey. I discuss why these letters are so compelling and the themes that very quickly surfaced from the hundreds of responses I received. I share how these letters can increase respect, collaboration, and productivity in the workplace, in schools, and in your personal life, and how this year taught me what being mindful really means.

You don't have to wait until the end of the book to get started. Each chapter concludes with the sections "Consider This" and "For Your Journey," which give ideas and action steps to guide you on your own path. Throughout the book I provide ideas for creating your own list of lucky recipients. And in chapter 10, you'll find a simple recipe of three ingredients for writing compelling letters of your own so you can be part of this movement to build an explosive surge of kindness one letter at a time.

I developed The Power of *A Few Kind Words* into a workshop, and have had the privilege of being hosted in private homes, businesses, nonprofits, churches, and schools where I encourage participants of all ages and walks of life to pay attention to their relationships—our most valuable asset. We need one another. Authentic appreciations settle in your core and stay. They become words to be retrieved during a difficult time or revisited to feel cherished once again. Imagine if everyone wrote just one letter. A community of people feeling valued could be unstoppable.

My life coaching career has reinforced for me that we all have in common a shared humanity. We are more alike than we are different. We want to know someone notices us and that we deserve a seat at the table. We want to know we're not alone or invisible. Every single one of us can feel more present, connected, and purposeful when we choose to simply share our kind thoughts. This positivity practice offers us a way to take back a little control in a world that at times can seem chaotic.

Although society seems to share judgmental thoughts more freely than loving ones, I believe there is power in numbers and together we can make a seismic shift towards positivity, respect, and love. Every day we are provided with ample opportunities to make choices that can bring us closer to becoming our best selves and contribute to the greater good. We can share with those we love, appreciate, and admire what makes them special, or… we can keep it to ourselves.

My mission is to let people everywhere know they matter through writing unexpected letters of appreciation. Will you join me? It feels really great—I promise.

Chapter 1

My Dad and His Simple Request

———————————

THE TYPE OF love I felt for and received from my dad, Buzz Willis, was like that all-consuming, nonjudgmental, unconditional love you feel from your exuberant, tail-wagging dog. I felt safe, happy, and content when I was with him. I never questioned his love for me. It was simply there, as constant as the sounds of the peepers on a hot Long Island summer night where I grew up. Dad and I were just connected. It was an effortless, joyful relationship that was like a sandwich, love in the middle with hysterical laughing attacks on one side and bear hugs on the other. I was Daddy's little girl. I was his defender to the end, and he was my knight in shining armor.

Whatever he did, I wanted to do. If he was mowing the lawn, I was behind him with the clippers, trimming grass around the stairs in our backyard. If he was collecting kindling, I was too. If he wanted to go out on our Sunfish with the green and white striped sail, I was game. If he was watching golf, I was cheering on his favorite player (and, of course, mine), Arnold Palmer.

To this day, fall is my favorite season. Maybe it's nostalgia but raking leaves with Dad is right up there with my happiest childhood memories. Dad would be in his old brown suede bomber jacket and worn tan corduroy pants raking up enormous piles of leaves around the property. I was right behind him with my little kid's rake. Once the piles were "ready," Dad would take turns throwing my sister Wendy and me into them. We would completely vanish beneath the dry crinkling leaves and fight our way back to the top, begging Dad to throw us again. Seriously, there was nothing better. When we were done, and had raked the scattered leaves back into a big pile, Dad would light them on fire. Back in the day before the town ordinances prohibited burning, we would stand around the blaze, breathe in the smoky scent, and watch our pile disappear.

Dad was generous and spontaneous with his enormous bear hugs. He had the longest arms, and he would smoosh us together until we became one and I could smell the hair tonic he used to smooth his hair. When I was little, I would stand on his feet and wrap my arms around his long thin legs. He would dance me around the house as I hung on for dear life, laughing with delight.

When I grew older, we became co-conspirators. During my senior year of high school, I talked my parents into letting me host a big Saturday night party after a football game. (This was exactly the type of party I would never have allowed our kids to host!) It was an "open" party, so there was no telling how many people might show up. After begging and pleading for days, I finally wore my strict mother out and she agreed, under one condition: no drinking. I dutifully promised there would be no alcohol and promptly told my friends to hide the keg in the woods. The morning after the party Dad woke me up very early, saying, "We have a lot of cleaning up to do before your mother wakes up!" Together we collected garbage bags full of empty beer cans, and to this day, I have no idea what Dad did with the keg in the woods. When Mom got up, she surveyed the house and property and said, "See, I told you that you could have a successful, fun party without alcohol." I couldn't look at Dad for fear of bursting into hysterics. Don't get me wrong: Dad was not pleased with me at all, but I knew deep in my bones that he would keep my confidence. This was only one of the countless times I felt grateful to be supported and loved so unconditionally.

He was a man of few words, but those words were always supportive, positive, and nurturing. He possessed a heart of gold and the gift of listening. I can still feel his 6'2" body squeezed next to me on my twin bed with the orange and yellow swirled bedspread, his arms around me while I cried my eyes out over some boyfriend. He soaked up some of my despair and his quiet calm washed over me. It's simply amazing to me that Dad never judged anyone. No matter how much his household of girls tried to get him to engage in gossip, he would not participate. It seemed that being nonjudgmental was baked into his

DNA. Dad never preached to us about the importance of kindness and compassion, he just modeled it for us day in and day out.

He was the first up every morning along with our dog Smoochie, and later our dog Cuddles, who was born on Valentine's Day. In his blue terrycloth bathrobe and leather slippers, Dad would make the coffee and set the table with serrated grapefruit spoons and bowls for cereal. He would cut half a grapefruit for each of us, put it in a textured yellow bowl designed to match the fruit, sprinkle it with white sugar, and put out our selection of healthy cereal choices—Cap'n Crunch and Fruit Loops—all while drinking his black coffee and smoking his first Pall Mall of the day.

When I turned eleven, I advanced to Corn Flakes and promptly fell in love for the first time. The model on the Corn Flakes box captivated me! I would eat my cereal and stare at the gorgeous, dark-haired, green-eyed guy and tell Dad I was going to marry someone who looked just like that. When the box was empty, I cut out the photo of my dream man and taped him to my mirror. Dad affectionately named him the Corn Flakes Guy and for years would ask me how each of my crushes and dates compared to my Corn Flakes Guy. He humored me as, yet again, I described my big white wedding in detail and talked about how wonderful it would be when he walked me down the aisle into the arms of my very own Corn Flakes Guy.

Dad wasn't perfect. He had one very annoying habit that drove the family insane. Whenever he was asked what he wanted for his birthday or Christmas he always said the same thing: "A few kind words." That frustrated us so much because we didn't know how to buy a few kind words and wrap them up in a box. So instead, I'd buy him a tie with golden retrievers on it, golf tees, and a package of neon-color cigarette lighters.

When we were in college, Wendy and I got up early one Christmas morning and drove an hour to pick up a wiggly, adorable puppy to put under the tree for Dad. I thought asking for a few kind words was like asking for nothing. Wasn't gift giving the way we show someone we love them? Apparently not to my father. He had his own language of love. I woke every day to Dad offering a kiss and a cheery "time to get up." I never fell asleep until he poked his head into my bedroom and said, "I love you." He would have been so happy receiving lots of I love you's, but instead he got a four-legged friend he named Bogey after his most recent golf game.

But Then

On January 31, 1987, he was gone. Dad had a massive heart attack while playing tennis and winning in the second set. He was sixty-seven years old. I was twenty-four and newly engaged for four weeks to my Corn Flakes Guy. Dad would never get to walk me down the aisle and I would never get to give him *a few kind words*.

It's been thirty-six years since my mother called

with the unfathomable news on that Saturday morning. My fiancé, Tom, and I had separate apartments in Boston, as was done back in the mid-1980s, but he just happened to be over early that morning. The kitchen was filled with the smell of bacon sizzling in the pan, and I can remember the sound of eggs being cracked into a bowl when the phone rang. Tom went to answer it, but I yelled "Don't answer it! It may be my mother and you definitely shouldn't be here this early!"

I picked up the phone and heard Mom say, "Tracey?"

I covered the receiver with my hand, laughing with relief that Tom had not answered it. Then Mom said the three words that changed my life forever: "Honey, Daddy died."

Just like in the movies, I fell to my knees, screaming. I thrust the phone to Tom and entered a dark tunnel of shock, disbelief, adrenaline, and utter despair. I can remember clearly thinking, *He can't be gone because he has to walk me down the aisle on August 29th.* That was our plan.

I became simultaneously catatonic and frantic. That probably doesn't make any sense, but for those who've had the misfortune of losing a loved one suddenly, maybe it makes sense to you. My brain was so overwhelmed with those horrible words spinning around in my head that I shut down because that was all I was capable of. At the same time, I was overcome with the need to get home to my mother and Wendy in Long Island. But I had no ability to get off the floor.

With the most grace and love I can ever imagine, Tom stood me up and said, "Let's go pack." He guided me to the bedroom and as I stared into my closet, I just started sobbing at the prospect of packing for my father's funeral when he was supposed to be on the tennis court enjoying his regular Saturday morning game.

Dad hated black, so I grabbed a gray skirt and a bright peach sweater. Dad was everything bright and sparkly in my life and I can remember having that one coherent thought: I will not wear black to his funeral.

I wasn't the only person who loved Buzz. When I entered the church with my mother, brother, and sisters, I had to fight down the lump of gratitude when I saw the hundreds of friends and family from near and far who had come to celebrate our dad, who they knew as Buzz. I've had three experiences in my life that I'll never find quite the right words to describe, but have reinforced for me how our loved ones never really leave us. These experiences touched my soul and I consider them precious gifts. The first happened at Dad's funeral and the others I will share later in the book.

I'd written a eulogy because I simply had to. I sat up in the tiny bedroom in the house my parents moved to during my senior year in college. All that fit was a twin bed and a three-drawer dresser with flower knobs from my childhood. With a box of Kleenex and a photo of Dad by my side, I tried to put into words what unconditional love feels like. If you've ever written a eulogy you know about this struggle. How do you express in a few minutes a life-time of relationship? The youngest of his six children, I wrote from my heart, filled with a need to make sure all the attendees understood, from my twenty-four-year-old perspective, just how special my dad was.

Then, I realized: Writing the eulogy was the easy part. The larger problem was I didn't think I could stand up at the pulpit and read my love letter out loud. I was too emotional. So, I made an agreement with the minister that he would look at me when it was my turn, and I would either stand up or shake my head no and he would move on with the service.

Sitting in the front row with my family, know-ing all eyes were on our pew absorbing our pain, I decided I couldn't read my eulogy. And that's when it happened. A brilliant beam of light came through one of the gorgeous stained-glass windows that surround St. John's of Lattingtown Church and shone directly on me. It seemed to skip my mother and my fiancé, who were sitting on my left and right, but filled me with the most amazing warmth and sense of love. With absolute certainty, I sensed my father telling me he was alright, and I would be too. My words do not do this justice, but Dad lifted me up in the seconds before the minister looked at me and gave me the strength and determination to honor him with a few kind words. What he always wanted.

My sister and brother then shared the pulpit for their eulogy, which they actually titled, "A Few Kind Words," after Dad's mantra. They each shared some beautiful thoughts and then took turns reading words that were meaningful to Dad: family, friends, golf, tennis, dogs, vodka, pretzels—offering Dad a final rendition of a few kind words...or what we thought at the time Dad meant by those words.

An Unexpected Gift

The seven months between my father's sudden passing and my wedding day were a blurry mix of overwhelming grief and abundant joy. They were both an ending and a beginning. Mourning Dad and at the same time planning my dream wedding to my Corn Flakes Guy. It was a crapshoot every day which emotion would win out.

The first wedding task, after Mom and I could bear to shift gears back to wedding planning, was to change the wording on the engagement announcement written in my father's handwriting and still waiting on the kitchen table to be sent to the *Locust Valley Leader*, our local newspaper. We had to remove two words, a total of five letters, but the enormity of those five letters still makes me feel as if I can't breathe. Instead of saying "Mr. and Mrs. Charles Everett Willis, Jr. announce the engagement of their daughter, Tracey Lee," it would now read just "Mrs. Charles Everett Willis, Jr. announces..."

I shared with Dad so many times how magical it would be when we stood alone together in the back of the church with me clutching his arm as he escorted me down the aisle. Now, during those seven months I couldn't imagine how I would handle not having Dad by my side. I was so afraid of breaking down in that moment. My wonderful brother would walk me down the aisle instead.

On our wedding day, August 29, 1987, I woke up early and slipped out of the house before Mom and my bridesmaids woke up. I needed to feel Dad's presence on this special day, so I went to the cemetery. Dad is buried in his family plot in Roslyn Cemetery. He is surrounded by his parents, grandparents, aunts, and uncles. The plot is marked by four cornerstones, each measuring about one foot in diameter. I plunked myself down on the cornerstone nearest to Dad and began to talk to him. I was emotional and asked him to send me a sign to let me know he would be with me on my wedding day.

Not thirty seconds later a tall, lanky, middle-aged man with a combover came running across the cemetery. He was yelling at me, "Get off that headstone! How dare you desecrate the memory of someone who died by sitting on their headstone."

I jumped up and told the man, who I learned was the caretaker of the cemetery, "I would never sit on someone's headstone! This is the cornerstone of our family plot." The caretaker's countenance changed immediately. He apologized and abruptly walked away. I stood open-mouthed, staring at him as he retreated.

Then I looked back at Dad and started to feel the beginnings of a completely unexpected laughing attack. Before I could even process what had just happened, I found myself laughing out loud in the early morning of the quiet cemetery and wiping away happy tears. There's no question in my mind that Dad orchestrated that moment, lifting my sadness and replacing it with levity. With certainty again, I felt Dad's warmth wrap around me as we shared one more glorious laughing attack. When I arrived at the cemetery, I had been anxious and sad, but by the time I left, I was an excited bride with her father's blessing.

Consider This

Our relationships are the greatest determinant of our happiness. Don't take your relationships for granted. Nurture them, lift them up, and know that even when loved ones pass on, they never really leave you.

For Your Journey

Can you conjure up the person who makes you feel this unconditional love? If so, it's truly a blessing. And if no one comes to mind, consider being that person who offers exuberant, tail-wagging love to someone in your life.

My favorite photo of Dad and me, circa 1965

Chapter 2

The Gift of "A Few Kind Words"

"Unexpected kindness is the most powerful, least costly, and most underrated agent of human change."

—Bob Kerrey

A LL THESE YEARS later, I finally have clarity about what Dad was brave enough to ask for year after year when he asked for "a few kind words": appreciation, affirmation, respect, and love. It took nearly four decades of life experience as a wife, mother, grandmother, sister, daughter, community volunteer, alumni director, CASA (Court Appointed Special Advocate for foster children), friend, and life and wellness coach to fully embrace the magnitude of the gift he bequeathed to me, and which I now offer to you.

The gift is the understanding and acknowledgment that we all want to know we matter. It's as simple as that. When we do, we thrive.

Each of us can give this gift to ourselves and someone else by simply sharing our kind thoughts. When we do, the reward is priceless: a deeper connection to someone. Unfortunately, we rarely give this gift to ourselves or someone else. But as negativity, fear, and judgement have reached epic levels in our world, it's time to tap into this superpower and together create an explosion of kindness. Humanity is begging for it.

As I look back over the course of my life, I realize Dad and I share the same language of love: words of affirmation. For me, it's always been through the written word. I love the burst of energy I get when I write notes to others letting them know how important they are to me.

But I didn't connect the dots to Dad and his longing for "a few kind words" until January 2019 when Tom and I were flying across the country from our home in Pennington, New Jersey to Portland, Oregon, to meet our first grandchild.

Tom had his headphones on and was watching his favorite show, *Curb Your Enthusiasm*, and literally laughing out loud. He was guffawing so loudly the woman across the aisle leaned forward and waved at him to get his attention. I was sure she was going to tell Tom to quiet down, and I was cringing. Instead, she said, "What are you watching? I want to watch that, too!"

That's what was happening while I had an honest-to-God *aha!* moment flying over the Midwest. With my eyes closed and my head resting back on the headrest, I visualized holding our grandson Hudson in my arms, and I could feel my whole body relax. It was such a welcome relief from the stress and tension I had been feeling while navigating Mom's care and my PMR.

I began to have an emotional conversation in my mind with Dad, sharing with him the news that he was a great-grandfather again, and his youngest child was now a grandmother. I could see Dad's baby blue eyes twinkle with delight as I smiled in my center seat. I started to think about what activities in life brought me this feeling of peace and joy. I wanted to capture more of it and release what was not serving me well. Without hesitation, my answer was this: deeply and authentically connecting with people. A meaningful conversation with a bestie or the barista that closes the door on all the distractions and allows us each to be seen, even for just a few minutes, always makes me feel more alive and happier. My next thought surprised me in its clarity: I was going to write an unexpected letter of appreciation to a different person every day for one year.

In that moment, I knew my first letter would be to our grandson Hudson and my last letter would be to Dad. The other 363 letters would be a fun mystery to unravel. Writing 365 letters of appreciation sounded insanely daunting but felt strangely invigorating at the same time. This challenge would indeed give me the heavy dose of connection I craved.

Now let me be clear: goal-setting has never been my thing. I knew I had to say this challenge out loud to someone or it would just be another fleeting idea

I failed to grab hold of. It would've been easier to share it with the stranger sitting to my left because he'd never hold me accountable. Instead, I turned to Tom, lifted one side of his headphones off his ear, and shared my exciting challenge with him. He looked at me blankly and said, "That's great, honey," and then went back to the antics of Larry David. Even so, his reaction at that moment notwithstanding, Tom ended up being my most ardent supporter, as he's always been.

I said it out loud and now I had to own it.

I decided to call the project *"A Few Kind Words"* to give hundreds of other people the gift Dad always asked for. What I started at that moment turned into a legacy of love to my father with so many unexpected benefits to me and others. At the time, I didn't know the positive power that would be unleashed.

Consider This

The greatest gift we can give someone is to let them know they matter. When you help someone feel noticed by acknowledging what you appreciate about them, you're helping them thrive. Every one of us is deserving of being here. Sharing *A Few Kind Words* is like the first gooey bite of a perfectly cooked s'more......utterly delicious!

For Your Journey

Practice sharing a kind thought with the next person

who crosses your path. Either spoken or in writing. Don't make a big deal of it—just share the kind thought you're thinking and see how you feel. Try the concept on for size and start to get comfortable with it. Remember, practice makes improvement.

Chapter 3

365 People

---

*"I will save your note forever in my special
journal. I want my ancestors to find it and
read how fabulous I am. It made me cry and
I read it over and over."*

—Susan, letter recipient

THE FIRST QUESTION most people ask when they
hear about my yearlong journey is, "How do you
possibly know 365 people to write to?" Well, we all
can find 365 people to say something kind to if we
decide to make it a priority. You just have to slow
down, start paying attention, and notice the interac-
tions you have with friends, colleagues, family, and
random people throughout the day. There are gifts
waiting to be appreciated everywhere you look.

I started by making a list of all my closest family
and friends. Then I added people I worked with, vol-
unteered with, neighbors and community members.
I included people I didn't know well but wanted to
get to know better. I added friends from elementary

school, middle school, high school, and college, and even my parents' friends.

The most fun group actually were the people I didn't know but had a positive interaction with, like Scott, who worked at our local pharmacy and who always had the most welcoming smile and hearty greeting. Our family had named him "Smiley Guy" for years, but I'd never told him how much I enjoyed going into his store simply because of the way his whole being lit up when he greeted me or any customer.

I also wrote to the salesman at Best Buy who spent two hours helping me buy a new phone. Technology is not my thing, but this young man with a beard and a welcoming smile seamlessly combined patience with kindness. At the two-hour mark, I felt like I had a friend. He treated me with respect and gave me as much of his time as I needed. He made me feel like I mattered, and I wanted him to feel the same in return, so I sent a letter to him at Best Buy. Tom should've written him a letter as well because he saved Tom hours of phone support with me!

I left letters for waiters who took good care of us, the barista at the new coffee shop, and the lovely woman who ran the jury room at the courthouse.

I wrote to our new dentist and his staff because I left my annual cleaning feeling like their office should be nominated for a customer service award. I got a handwritten note in return.

I loved writing to Steve, who runs the front desk at the senior community where my mother-in-law lives. The warmth with which he greets me every single time I arrive makes me feel special. His care for my mother-in-law and all our family is a beautiful thing to be part of. I wanted to make sure he knew that he made my day better every time I visited. After he read my letter, he told me he cried. It touched his heart. Now, three years later, he still mentions how special my letter is to him.

I even wrote to Maria Shriver and Oprah. I needed them to know how much the way they live their lives has guided how I live mine. Although the chances are slim to none that they ever actually held my letter in their hands, it felt wonderful to appreciate two women who are role models of compassionate living.

As my journey continued, I found myself intentionally engaging in more conversations with people I knew, those I wanted to know better, and those I didn't know at all. I was asking more questions and I was listening more. I was feeling more connected to my community, near and far, and I was completely energized. Finding 365 letter recipients became no problem at all.

> **Never assume a person already knows**
> **you appreciate them. Appreciations are**
> **fuel that help us be our best selves.**

What I choose to believe is we all have kind thoughts most days, although most of the time we do nothing with them. We allow them to pass through us and fly away as missed opportunities for connection.

What I did, and what I encourage you to try, is capture those kind thoughts in writing and don't waste them.

When someone tells you they love what you're wearing, you carry that compliment with you all day.

When your boss or a colleague compliments you on your presentation or the way you handled a discussion, you are energized in the best possible way.

Now, imagine if those compliments were shared in writing. You can write on a Post-it Note or monogrammed stationery. It doesn't matter. The type of paper is meaningless. The message is everything. That note becomes a keepsake.. Don't deprive someone of your appreciation. It makes a lasting impact.

Teresa's Thoughtful Gesture

Our delightful mail carrier, Teresa, gave our dog, Ella, a treat every day. Teresa had no idea she made not only Ella's day but Tom's and mine as well. As soon as Ella heard the mail truck in the neighborhood, she would fly off her chair, where she sat perched looking out the window, and run full speed into the kitchen, sliding on the laminate floor trying to stop before passing her doggie door. She'd regain her footing, bolt through the door just in time to bark an enthusiastic greeting and devour the treat Teresa threw onto the driveway. Watching this joyful routine between friends never got old. Teresa would return our wave of thanks with her broad smile and an enthusiastic wave of her own.

I needed to let her know how much her thoughtfulness impacted our household day after day, so Teresa found a letter addressed to her in our mailbox. That gesture has facilitated a lovely friendship filled with warm conversations around the mailbox. We share photos of our grandchildren and discuss travels we have taken. I look forward to getting a dose of Teresa's joyful energy as often as I can.

As I write this book, it's now a few years since our friendship began and Ella is sixteen years old. She's totally deaf and can no longer jump onto the chair and look out the window. She can't hear the mail truck coming and her vision is compromised by old age. One day, Teresa asked with concern if Ella was alright since she wasn't seeing her very often. I described her condition and Teresa replied, "Here's what I'll do. If I see your car in the driveway, I'll honk the horn, so you know to get Ella and bring her outside. I'll wait an extra minute. I want to make sure she gets her afternoon treat each day. I miss seeing her enthusiastic tail wag."

Teresa's demonstration of compassion touched me to the core. What she offered was so above and beyond her job description. Her generous gift of kindness was a brilliant reminder of what can happen when we nurture our relationships. So now I listen for the honk from the mail truck, fly off my chair to get Ella, and together we run outside for our treat.

A dog bone for Ella and a smile and a wave from a friend for me.

Consider This

There are people all around you just waiting to be appreciated. Those you know well and those you have limited interaction with. All you need to do is slow down, start noticing, ask questions, and listen. No more missed opportunities for connection!

For Your Journey

Start your own list of people you might consider surprising with an unexpected letter of appreciation. Who comes to mind first? Consider those closest to you, and don't forget those you don't know well but appreciate, admire, or respect from afar. If no one comes to mind yet that's OK. As you read this book, I'll offer suggestions that might get you thinking in ways you had not considered. The more you start noticing and engaging with those around you, the more people you'll find to add to your list.

Chapter 4

Stop Scrolling and Start Strolling

"Your 'A Few Kind Words' card has remained on my nightstand and makes me smile every time I read it."

—Colin, letter recipient

TAKE A MINUTE and think back to some of your fondest memories. Why are those memories so fond? I bet they involve feeling authentically connected to someone through a shared kindness or experience. Either something you did for someone, or someone did for you or with you. Which begs the question, why don't we create more opportunities for authentic connection and kindness? Are we really too busy? Are we too self-absorbed? Are we too afraid? Are we spending too much time lost in technology? Although social media is meant to help us feel more connected, it becomes isolating when overused. We can't improve our relationships if we don't make the effort to meaningfully connect.

How often do you come to a stoplight while driving and look over at the car beside you and see the driver checking their phone? Maybe you're checking your own phone. We're addicted to this low-level consumption. The thirty-second stoplight cycle provides yet another opportunity for this constant distraction. We've forgotten how to just be in the moment.

Don't you love to see a driver singing with abandon and slamming his steering wheel to the beat of a favorite song rather than getting honked at because he hasn't looked up from his phone to see the light turned green? It's much more difficult to find what you appreciate about your surroundings and the people in those surroundings if you're constantly distracted by your phone. You can't act, change, or grow if you don't first become aware.

> I challenge you to stop scrolling and start strolling. Put your phone down, look up from your computers, get out of your chair, make eye contact, and ask open-ended questions... then listen for the answers.

Learn something new about the people you already know well and the people you don't know at all. Adopting an inquisitive attitude shows people you're interested in them and is a sign of respect, with the bonus that it's fun to engage. We all love stories, and we all have stories to tell.

I'll never forget learning that the man who ran buildings and grounds at the school I was working for had a passion for ballroom dancing! I wouldn't have guessed that in a million years if I hadn't engaged him in conversation one day by asking him what he did over the weekend. He happily shared that he and his wife regularly participate in ballroom dancing competitions, and they'd spent the weekend practicing. That one question I asked provided for wonderful ongoing conversations.

Allow people to surprise you. Your daily life will become more interesting and more vivid. Sometimes, people may not wish to engage and that's OK. At least you made them feel noticed.

Tom and I are *Jeopardy* watchers now. Our favorite part is hearing what the contestants choose to share about themselves when giving their one-minute introductions. Often, they're very random things, like the contestant who shared that she has a collection of KitKat bars from around the world. Her favorite comes from Japan and she can only get them in specific regions and train stations. They are Okinawa Sweet Potato KitKat bars. Who knew! If I was on the show, my interesting fact would be that for every single night of our thirty-six-year marriage, Tom and I have switched the side of the bed we sleep on. Our first bedroom was so tiny the bed was pushed up against a wall. We didn't think it was fair that someone had to crawl over the other if you had to get up in the night, so we just started switching and have never stopped this rotation, whether at home or on vacation. We do have to pass each other our books each night but it's just part of our routine. We have yet to find any other couple who does this!

What riveting fact would you share about yourself if you were on *Jeopardy*? Ask other people what their riveting fact would be. Get the conversation going.

Being interested in another human being you're sharing space with is one of the kindest things you can do.

We're not meant to live in isolation. Our relationships are the greatest determinant of our happiness. Dr. Mark Hyman, international leader in the field of functional medicine, says, "Perhaps the most important thing to do to keep your brain happy is to make time for your relationships. Happy relationships are key to a healthy life. We know now that those with strong social connections benefit mentally, emotionally, and physically—with decreased all-cause mortality compared to those who are socially isolated."[4]

Consider proactively creating an environment that allows for connection and appreciations to show up. Go on a story hunt. This might mean leaving your phone in the car when you go into the coffee shop so that you're more likely to strike up a conversation with the barista or someone in line. Try taking a walk and leaving all technology behind. As you notice your surroundings with new focus you make space for creativity, inspiration, and curiosity to breathe. You might even meet a new neighbor.

Think about times when you had a really good conversation with someone.

By good, I mean reciprocal, deep, meaningful.

How did you feel? Did you feel heard and that you mattered to them? Did you leave that conversation with an uptick in positive energy? As Marisa G. Franco, PhD, says in her book *Platonic*, "Every time you make a friend, someone else does, too." Authentic connection is way more energizing and sustaining than the caffeine buzz a cup of coffee gives you or the sugar rush you get from eating an entire sharing-size bag of peanut M&Ms by yourself. I know this from personal experience.

I believe there is magic in kindness: It's empowering, energizing, accessible to everyone, and naturally contagious. Can you think of anything else that elicits that sort of emotional response every single time you experience it or observe it? I can't. Regardless of your age, gender, income, job, or nationality, kindness resonates. Mark Twain said it best: "Kindness is the language that the deaf can hear and the blind can see." You don't have to speak the same language to convey it. It's a universally understood feeling that has the power to soften hearts and bring you immediately into the present moment. Acknowledging each other is a supreme act of kindness. I spent the year engaging in intentional conversation, asking questions, listening, and learning. Indeed, my happiness level increased as I felt more connected or reconnected to every single person I wrote to.

Cynthia and the Best Chai Latte Ever

I walked into the new coffee shop at the end of the row of stores on Main Street. The simple temporary sign said Éclair Bakery in turquoise lettering above the door. I'd been impatiently waiting for them to open as I didn't love the chai lattes offered at the two other shops in town. Those chai lattes were too spicy for my taste. I longed for a mixture of sweet and frothy.

I entered the small narrow shop with bay windows on either side of the door that allowed for cozy seating and sidewalk watching and was happy to see there were four people in line ahead of me. I wanted this coffee shop to thrive as it was within walking distance of our home. I was surprised to see the woman behind the counter was probably in her sixties and not a young hipster barista. This woman was moving very methodically and not making much conversation with the clients.

When there was only one person ahead of me, I glanced up at the large blackboard with menu options written in pastel-color block print. To my dismay, I did not see chai latte listed. As the gentleman ahead of me picked up his double espresso with almond milk, I said to the barista, "Please tell me you have chai latte?"

After an uncomfortable pause with her gazing directly at me she said, "Well, yes we do and I'm going to make you the best chai latte you've ever had!"

I was so taken aback by her confident reply that I

responded with the first thing that came to my mind: "Well that's a ballsy statement, game on!"

She turned around and pulled out the chai and asked me what type of milk I wanted. When I told her oat milk, she said "Good choice."

We proceeded to banter back and forth as she poured a little of this and stirred a little of that, frothed the milk, and finished with a flourish of ground cinnamon. She slowly turned around, looked me directly in the eyes once again, plunked the to-go cup down on the counter, and slid it toward me, motioning me to take a sip.

I first brought the cup to my nose to see if I detected a spicy smell and breathed in a sweet aroma. With our eyes locked, I took one sip and then another.

"She's right," I proclaimed for those in line behind me who had become invested in this unexpected chai latte challenge. "This is, indeed, the best chai latte I've ever had!"

She replied with a smile and shrug of her shoulders, "I told you so!"

I asked her for her name. She answered, "Cynthia," and I expressed my profound gratitude and promised to be back.

Sipping my steaming cup of deliciousness, I walked down the street toward home, smiling as I realized my quest for the perfect chai latte was over. I replayed the delightful and unexpected exchange and realized I had an extra skip in my step. In Cynthia's reserved and funny way, she totally engaged me and made me want to come back. Not just because she made the best chai latte, but also because I enjoyed the unexpected connection. Without a second thought I knew Cynthia would be my letter recipient of the day. I wanted her to know I left the shop more joyful than when I had arrived.

I stopped at the coffee shop the next day to hand deliver my letter to Cynthia. I was disappointed to find she wasn't working that day. I left the letter with the owner, making her promise me she would hand it personally to Cynthia.

I wasn't able to go back for another two weeks. When I walked in, Cynthia's back was to me as she was making an espresso for a young man. Without turning around, she said over her shoulder, "What'll you have?"

I replied, "The best chai latte ever."

With that, Cynthia stopped mid-brew and turned around. Her eyes instantly glistened with tears. She said, "No one has ever done that for me before and I've been doing this for a very long time. Your letter is on my dresser at home, and I've read it every day before coming to work." Then she walked around the counter, wrapped her arms around me, and gave me one of the most memorable long, tight hugs of my life (this was pre-Covid). She said, "You made not only my day, but my week, my month and year. Thank you."-

I left the store feeling filled to the brim with gratitude. The reason wasn't just in the warm cup with the sweet aroma I was holding. I was so glad I had taken a few minutes to share my kind thoughts with Cynthia. I had a new friend, and it was going to be a good day. Over time, I learned we were both caring for our elderly mothers. I would start my weekly trip to visit Mom with a stop at Éclair Bakery. Cynthia and I would share our mother updates and I would leave the coffee shop with the best chai latte ever and a lifted spirit infused with the kindness and mutual understanding of my friend Cynthia.

Consider This

Stop scrolling, start strolling, and go on a story hunt. This will allow you to connect with people in a more profound way. My experience is that most people are inherently kind and relish the opportunity to let that shine. Sometimes they just need to be prodded. Being interested in another human being you're sharing space with is one of the kindest things you can do.

For Your Journey

Going on a story hunt is an easy, fun, and kind way to begin to engage in your community. Select a day over the next week when you'll ask one open-ended question to a few people you interact with. You don't have to ask everyone the same question; just ask something that requires more than a fine, good, yes, or no response. Here are a few ideas:

- What made you want to work here?
- What is the best part of your day?
- What riveting fact about yourself would you share on *Jeopardy*?

Consider trying one of my favorite things to do: Buy a coffee or a chai for the person in line behind you. I promise you both will leave happier than when you entered, and you'll have a story to share. At the end of the day, check your energy level. Are you more energized because you interacted with intention? The more you get to know someone, the more you can find to appreciate about them.

Chapter 5

Handwritten Notes Will Never Get Lost in the Cloud

"Real letters are becoming a rarity today and I'll treasure this one always. I'll put it somewhere I can reread it when I need a lift."

—Linda S., letter recipient

"I'm saving your letter in my box to be read as my eulogy and for my kids to read. I loved it and it was so unexpected."

—Gretchen, letter recipient

THE SECOND MOST common question people ask in bewilderment when they hear about my journey is, "How did you find all of those addresses?" Then they usually follow this up with, "I don't even have stamps."

When I present my workshop, or just talk about it with interested people, they get thrown by the fact I was writing and mailing handwritten notes. Although people like to call letter writing a lost art, I believe the handwritten letter will never go out of style. Technology is constantly changing but the handwritten note has a beautiful permanence that can outlast any email, WhatsApp, or text message.

It seems that it isn't the letter content that causes people the most angst, but the mechanics behind finding a piece of stationery, a pen, an address, and stamp. Then you have to physically mail it through snail mail. Millennials and Gen Zers think I'm speaking a different language. No auto-correct for spelling, no emoji to express how you feel, and no send button.

You do have to put a little bit of effort into sharing unexpected letters of appreciation—handwrite them and use words to express your feelings! Any type of paper works. The paper is just the vehicle to convey the message. Printer paper works just fine. As far as finding an address, a little sleuth work is all it takes. Try whitepages.com, Google, phone a friend, look up an organization directory or just ask. You can do this!

My neighbor Chuck wrote a wonderful letter to his grandchildren titled "Why a Letter." These are two of my favorite and poignant reflections:

1. "The difference between a text and a handwritten note is the difference between a handshake and a hug. A handshake and a hug are both signs of friendship, but the hug touches the soul a little more deeply."

2. "You only have to ask yourself this question to appreciate the depth of a handwritten note: Would you rather be told Congratulations, or I Love You in a text or a handwritten letter?"

The Unexpected Benefits of Letter Writing[5]

---

1. Writing a letter makes you happier

In 2012, the Journal of Happiness Studies published a study where Stephen Toepfler et al looked at the effects of writing letters of gratitude. They found that it increased the happiness and life satisfaction of those who took part. And interestingly, the more letter writing people did over the three weeks of the study, the happier and more satisfied they were.[6]

2. A letter can be cherished

You can't keep a WhatsApp message, and yes, while you might keep an email, honestly, how many have you ever actually printed out? But a letter is different; it has the same magic quality as a photo.

3. It's a simple way to be mindful

Writing a letter is different, it requires a great deal more thoughtfulness. It lets you pause, take yourself away from a screen, and get some time out to think about what you would like to say. It's a simple way to have a moment of mindfulness.

4. It is a hug in an envelope to loved ones...

Penning a handwritten letter makes you feel significantly more emotionally engaged with the person you are writing to, than if you simply sent an email or text. Far greater connection than a digital message.

5. ... And a token of kindness to strangers

If you don't have anyone you want to write to this weekend, why not spread some sunshine and write to a stranger?

What's Inside Your Mailbox?

Imagine going to your mailbox and among the bills and the circulars you find a handwritten letter addressed to you, and it's not your birthday or a holiday. Nothing monumental has happened in your life that would warrant a letter. You open it up and someone has taken the time to write you a note filled with reasons why they admire, appreciate, and maybe even love you.

Here are some things that are likely to happen: You'll read the letter more than once; you'll save the letter; and you're likely to share the letter. Some of you will even tear up. Your mood will change for the better and for a few minutes you will become fully present.

Recall if you've been lucky enough to have received an unexpected handwritten letter of appreciation. I bet you still have it in your file for keepsakes. How many emails or text messages have you saved that made you feel good?

Considering how infrequently people report writing or receiving handwritten letters in our digital age, I was fascinated by a survey of 2,000 adults conducted by handwritten note service Bond that reported: "81 percent of Americans consider a handwritten note to feel more meaningful than email or text, with millennials, surprisingly, leading the pack. Nearly nine in ten (87 percent) millennials value handwritten notes more than alternative means of communication."[7]

Unique Handwriting

There's something deeply nostalgic about recognizing someone's handwriting. All of us have handwriting that's one-of-a-kind. It's part of our beautiful identity.

I bet you can conjure up the handwriting of your parents, siblings, spouse, children, and best friend. It's a visceral connection to them you'll always feel when you see an envelope addressed to you in their handwriting.

Wendy and I always had to decipher our mother's left-handed, loopy, slanted cursive writing for our teachers whenever she sent a note to school. But to us, it was totally legible and like a fingerprint, uniquely Mom. The Times New Roman or Calibri font your loved one chose when they wrote you an email just doesn't conjure up the same emotional response.

The act of writing with my favorite blue pen is sort of mesmerizing. Rather than banging out my thoughts on a keyboard or typing on my tiny smartphone with only thumbs, picking up a pen that glides smoothly across the paper and taking time to form my letters into words is centering. Knowing my letter recipient is going to physically hold in their hands something I held in my hands makes me feel like my gratitude for them is sealed within the paper and adds to the connection. I think that's my favorite part of writing these letters. They are a tangible expression of kindness that touches both parties.

During my "note-a-day" year, I kept notecards in my purse, in the car, and of course at home. I tried to get into a routine of writing my note in the morning, but that never really stuck. I wrote when the mood struck—morning, noon, or night. In the car, in the house, in my mother's assisted living apartment, in a hotel, in a restaurant, and even at the beach. I was indifferent to the venue. Being able to become mindfully present was everything.

One of the first letters I wrote was to our server at the Rocky Hill Inn in Rocky Hill, New Jersey. It was a chaotic, packed restaurant and we were seated right next to the kitchen with the door swinging both ways every minute or so as servers rushed by. But our server made us feel like we were the only customers in the crowded restaurant. She gave us her undivided attention and asked us questions that made us feel like she cared.

When we got into the car after dinner, I decided she would be getting my letter for the day. I wasn't yet carrying stationery with me, so I wrote my appreciations on a piece of Tom's company letterhead that happened to be in the car, sealed the letter, and ran it back inside and left it on our table.

To this day, I cringe thinking she must have thought she was the recipient of one of those surprise huge tips. Instead, she was the recipient of *a few kind words…* priceless.

When you handwrite, you are engaging in a slower, more thoughtful form of communicating. You are potentially writing something that someone's children and grandchildren will have the pleasure of reading. The handwritten note can transcend generations. It won't get lost in the Cloud when the technology changes from one decade to the next, but it may be found in someone's special box years later or bound in a leather scrapbook on the top shelf of a bedroom closet.

Kay's Love Letters

I had a special friendship with an elderly woman named Kay from our church. She was widowed when she was in her sixties, had no children, and was legally blind due to macular degeneration. I met her when she was eighty and had the pleasure of being her friend until she passed away at 100.

Kay was tiny and spritely and made friends more easily than anyone I've ever met. She had an inquisitiveness and a delight for life that was contagious and endearing. She dressed in bright colors and wild patterns and had an impressive collection of costume jewelry to embellish each outfit. Although she may have had limited eyesight, what she did have in abundance was the purest example of faith I've ever been exposed to and a relationship with her husband Larry that was one of the greatest love stories I was privileged to witness. I'm a romantic at heart. Kay and Larry's adoration for one another transcended what I saw at the movies or read in my romance novels. I never met Larry, but I felt like I knew him intimately through his precious love letters.

Kay had bound Larry's letters in two green leather scrapbooks she kept safe on the top shelf of her bedroom closet. There must have been a hundred letters from the 1940s until his death in 1984. After Kay and I chatted about life, faith, and love while sipping tea from her gold-rimmed teacups, she would ask if I could stay a few minutes longer and read her a couple of Larry's letters. Being legally blind, she could no longer read them herself.

Kay trusted me enough to let me share in the most intimate relationship of her life. He was older than she was, and they courted for seven years until he felt he was deserving of her hand. Larry wrote in both flowery prose and simple expressions of love. He was tender, romantic, funny, and so open with his adoration for Kay. He always referred to himself as "S. F." standing for sentimental fool and his salutations were always loving and creative. My favorite being Dear Splendelicious One! He ended many of his letters making up an acronym that Kay would have to decipher for me as she laughed her sweet laughter and remembered.

Some of the letters were written in beautiful now vintage Hallmark cards embossed in velvet and glitter. They were for holidays like Valentine's Day, always St. Patrick's Day because Kay's favorite color was green, Thanksgiving, and Christmas. She would listen to my voice with rapt attention, and I could see her drift back into the past and feel the depth of Larry's love wrapping warmly around her like the gorgeous mink stole he surprised her with one birthday—and that now keeps me warm.

Larry could never have imagined when he wrote

to the love of his life that someone he never met would be reading his love letters to his wife decades later. But those letters were a gift to me as well as to Kay because Larry's letters were like taking a master class in what love looks like in its purest form. These letters sustained Kay over the decades after he passed. While she lived more of her life without him by her side than she did with him, he was always in her heart. Those letters in the leatherbound books, which brought him back to life, were her most treasured possessions. I would often leave her sitting on her beige damask loveseat lost in another time with her letters on her lap, Larry's voice refreshed in her memory, and I know they were dancing together in the kitchen.

Consider This

There is something profoundly special about a handwritten letter you can hold in your hand. It shows that someone chose to be very intentional when they wrote to you. You mattered enough for that person to slow down and think about you. They selected the paper or card they wanted to use, found your address and a stamp, and then went to the post office or nearest mailbox. Knowing your letter recipient is going to actually hold in their hands something you held in your hands seals in the gratitude. Handwriting is very nostalgic.

For Your Journey

Build your toolkit:

- Have a supply of stationery, notecards, or Post-it notes at home, in your car, your desk, and maybe even your purse so you aren't scrambling to find something to write on.
- Find the type of pen that you really like. Then, buy a bunch of them.
- Go to the post office or stamps.com (let's collectively keep the Post Office in business!) and buy a supply of postage stamps so you can send the letters at any time.
- Cultivate an attitude of gratitude so you are open to seeing the good in those around you.

Chapter 6

You Made My Day...

"Thanks for making my day!! I have read your letter three times and I have a huge smile on my face. Again, you really made my day!!"

—Pam, letter recipient

"Receiving your amazing letter really made my day. It arrived at the perfect time and with the right messages that brought my energy way up! Thank you!"

—Romy, letter recipient

I STARTED THIS challenge to make me feel better. I never expected to hear back from the letter recipients. The act of writing the letters was the elixir I needed. I wrote from the heart just wanting someone to know I'd had a kind thought about them. When you write your own letters of appreciation, I encourage you to write from a place of giving rather than having any expectation of receiving. Practicing the art of action without expectation is liberating. The beautiful byproduct of this journey is that I did hear back from 241 out of the 365 letter recipients, and their kind words to me kept the circle of appreciation growing larger and larger.

It wasn't long into my journey that two themes started to emerge. The first one was that I was hearing the exact same words over and over: *You made my day.* The crazy thing is that writing the letter had already made my day before it made theirs. It appeared the good feelings being generated were multiplying. To have well over 150 letter recipients say the exact same words was astonishing, humbling, and eye-opening.

All I was doing, from my perspective, was having a kind thought about someone, taking a notecard, and sharing my thoughts. I was not writing a term paper about them, just letting them know what I appreciated about them, and my little notes were exponentially changing the energy around their days. If my notes were having such a profound effect, then that means there is a real dearth of appreciations being shared. People rarely receive notes like the ones I was sending, and the impact is more significant than we might think. What started as a journey to make me feel empowered, energized, and uplifted was making the letter recipients feel the exact same things.

Wouldn't you like to have your day made and at the same time make someone else's day? I can tell you from personal experience, jotting down your nice thoughts on any handy piece of paper and sending or hand-delivering those thoughts is a recipe that is easy to follow and equally easy to digest. Since you already had the kind thought, the hard part is done. All you need to do is transpose the thought into writing and send it off. I think you'll like how you feel and who you're being when you incorporate this practice into your life. Give it a try and see for yourself.

Meeting Ms. Davis

I received my jury duty notice and, like most people, wasn't that excited to have to put a week on hold while waiting to see if I was called to duty. I was summoned to the Mercer County Court House on the second day. When I got to the jury room, I had to check in with one of two women sitting behind a big brown desk in the front of a large room with about 150 moderately comfortable chairs. She scanned the barcode on my jury notice and then did the most unexpected thing. She looked me in the eyes and said, "Good morning, Tracey. We're so happy to see you this morning. Please take a seat anywhere in the room and after everyone is checked in, we'll tell you how the day will unfold."

Dale Carnegie nailed it when he said, "A person's name is to him or her the sweetest and most important sound in any language." I certainly didn't expect to feel so welcome while standing in a cattle call line with 150 people.

I chose to sit near the front of the room, and I watched the two women as they checked people in. They addressed every single person by name and used great eye contact.

When everyone was finally seated, one of the women stood up and told us how the jury process would work. Once again, I was pleasantly surprised. I found myself laughing and listening with my full attention. This lovely lady was a wonderful mixture of kind, appreciative, and funny. Laughing was not something I expected to be doing at the Mercer County Court House. She told us how much she appreciated our time and acknowledged that this was an interruption to everyone's schedule. We were reminded it was a privilege and our right to serve on a jury. She then told us we had to make sure to come back into this room to check out with them after we were dismissed from our jury. If we didn't, we would be arrested! She was warm and welcoming, and then told us that she had done this job for twenty-eight years. The fact that she was exuding joy after doing the same job for such a long time is what really captivated me.

She seemed to love her job and she showed it. I was having these kind thoughts about her, and I decided she would be my letter recipient for the day. When she wasn't looking, I asked the other woman for her name and was told it was Ms. Davis.

I took a notecard out of my purse, and while waiting to be called for my jury, wrote an unexpected letter of appreciation to Ms. Davis. I slipped it onto her desk unseen before leaving the main room.

I was dismissed from my jury the following day and because I didn't want to be arrested, went back to the jury room to check out. The same two women

were seated at the desk. Ms. Davis was helping some-
one else, so I went to the other woman. When she
scanned my barcode, she looked up and said, "Wait
a minute." Apparently, Ms. Davis had asked her col-
league to be on the lookout for me. She turned to
Ms. Davis, who then stood up and motioned for me
to meet her in front of the desk.

What happened next will stay with me for the rest
of my life. With the next day's group of jurors watch-
ing, Ms. Davis gave me another of those pre-pandemic
long, tight hugs. She then proceeded to say the same
words that Cynthia had said to me: "No one has ever
done that for me before and you made not only my
day, but my week, my month and my year." She told
me that she read the letter to her family that night
at the dinner table and that she's now going to keep
notecards in her purse and pay it forward. I left the
Mercer County Court House with the biggest smile
on my face. I felt energized and happy that I'd taken
the time to share my kind thoughts. What a missed
opportunity it would have been if I had kept them to
myself. My choice to send them out into the world
felt expansive!

Reconnecting...

While writing this chapter I had the overwhelm-
ing need to reconnect with Ms. Davis and thank her
again, more than three years later, for the way she
made me feel that day in March of 2019. I had no idea

if she was still working in the jury room at the Mercer County Court House, or if she would even remember me and our brief connection.

I had shared her heartwarming story at countless workshops over the years and Ms. Davis had become a special person to me. I googled the Mercer County Court House-Jury Duty and began navigating their website for information. I found an email address on the jury page and emailed my request, leaving all my contact information to be passed along to Ms. Davis if she indeed still worked there.

It was a long shot and I had little confidence we would be reconnected—until my phone rang a few hours later. "I hear you're looking for me, this is Ms. Davis."

It was like a shot of joy.

She told me she just happened to be on email duty that day and she was the one who actually read my email. I exclaimed, "Ms. Davis, I am so happy to hear your voice!"

I asked her if she remembered me, and she said, "Of course, I remember you. You touched my heart, and you're one of the nicest people I've met."

What she said next stunned me. "I've had so many people come through the jury room asking for me because they heard your story. Your letter has been hanging on my office wall and I show it to everyone who asks. When we were sent home because of the pandemic we were told to take home everything that was important to us since we had no idea how long we would be closed. Of course, I took your letter and since the pandemic it has been displayed on my wall at home with photos of all my grandchildren."

I had tears. We talked for about twenty minutes, and I learned that Ms. Davis has four birth children and five adopted children and seventeen grandchildren. Her big, warm, wonderful heart was evident to me in our brief interlude three years before, and learning of her large extended family only reinforced for me that my instincts were right.

Ms. Davis told me, "I treat people how I want to be treated. Most people don't want to be called for jury duty and I appreciate all of them." It was that innate kindness that once again reached out and drew me in. Our conversation was comfortable and filled with positive upbeat energy. I was instantly reminded why I felt compelled to write my unexpected letter of appreciation to her way back when because I felt the same warm, fuzzy feeling talking to her that day.

I'm sure I'm not the first person called for jury duty who had nice thoughts about this kind woman, but apparently I'm the only one to have written her a note letting her know she made a difference in my day.

Our story continued as I was selected to be on a jury in the final week of writing this book. I found Ms. Davis on the second floor of the Mercer County Court House and we had another joyful reunion complete with tight hugs and appreciation. Ms. Davis will be retiring at the end of this year after thirty-two years in a job where she made a difference for over three decades. I will always be grateful I was called for jury duty that day and our paths crossed. I know Ms. Davis will keep shining her brilliant light wherever she goes.

My letter to Ms. Davis:

———

Dear Ms. Davis,

You are delightful! Thank you for making the jury room a happy place. Every day for one year I am writing a letter of appreciation to a different person. You are my person today.

You clearly love what you do. After 28 years, I sure hope so! Your warmth, your smile and your fabulous sense of humor make us all feel welcomed. That is a gift that we don't come across often enough in this world. You are in the right job.

While it is a privilege to serve on a jury, we come into this room not sure what to expect. You and your lovely colleague treated us with respect and kindness.

While I don't know you at all... what I do know for sure is that you are a bright light in this world, and you are making a difference in this courthouse. Keep smiling and making people laugh!

With gratitude and appreciation,
Tracey Gates

———

Consider This

Over and over again, my letter recipients said the same thing to me: "You made my day." What an unexpected privilege it is to make someone's day. Don't underestimate the power of your words. The feel-good feelings are contagious. The act of sharing your kind thoughts just might make your day before it makes theirs!

For Your Journey

Go ahead and make someone's day. What are you waiting for? If you want to feel connected and do something meaningful then write someone an unexpected letter of appreciation. Picture a big smile on your person's face. The kind of smile that can't be held back but must be released, which then makes the eyes twinkle. Your words have the potential to make that happen.

Chapter 7

I Was Having a Really Bad Day...

"Thank you for your beautiful note. Without knowing it, your timing could not have been any better."

—Brian, letter recipient

"Sweet friend, thank you for my 'a few kind words.' Your timing was remarkable! And your words so touching... made my heart feel full and at a time I really needed it."

—Margie, letter recipient

ALMOST AS OFTEN as I heard *you made my day*, I was hearing the flipside. Countless people shared with me how they were in a bad place when they opened my letter of appreciation, but then their day changed for the better. They experienced an energy shift that sustained them for a little while. When I wrote my notes, I had no idea the recipients were in a bad place or were having a bad day. What was reinforced for me over and over is that we rarely really know what's going on in someone's life.

Every kind thought you have is a gift that has the potential to fill a void in another person's life.

You may think your kind thought has little value or that the person already knows what you are thinking or how you feel. Believe me, by not sharing your kind thought, you could be depriving that person of just the boost they need. No one ever tires of hearing they are noticed, valued, and that they matter. I've realized through my hundreds of letters and responses that people *crave* being noticed because sometimes we fear we're not worthy or lovable, or that we're not valued or seen. Together, let's help people be seen. Remember, your letter may arrive just at the moment someone needs to be lifted up, and you may just turn someone's day around!

Cara and the Ripple Effect

"I got your letter in the mail and the words of encouragement and blessing not only changed my day, that day, but it changed my view of my ability to move forward with my business. I was feeling very discouraged, and it came at the most opportune time and gave me the extra umph to keep going."

When Cara called to tell me my unexpected letter was a "blessing," something shifted. I consider a blessing to be something holy, revered, and life-enhancing. With Cara's message, I began to fully understand that our words have power far beyond what we might imagine.

I wrote to Cara seven weeks into my yearlong journey. I was feeling lifted up every single day when I put pen to paper, but it was Cara who helped me understand that kind thoughts hold healing powers in ways I hadn't yet fully embraced. They can be a blessing. I was humbled to have my words considered in that way.

Cara is an entrepreneur with a thriving jewelry-making business. She makes stunning necklaces out of antique horse brass and found objects (Carabrowndesigns.com). They are one-of-a-kind pieces that tell a story and carry on a legacy. She leads with her heart and makes this world more beautiful by her presence and her jewelry. What I didn't know at the time I wrote to her was that my unexpected letter of appreciation arrived right when another jeweler was emulating Cara's designs, without permission, and Cara was feeling really down. My words helped her reignite a belief in herself, and remind her of the reasons why she is such a gifted woman and entrepreneur.

Cara was inspired by my message to be intentional with our words because she believes, as I do, that our words can build up or tear down. In a deliberate effort to build people up, she invited me to speak to her book group and share my message and mission. Seven of us sat around a gorgeous farm table in her eighteenth-century home—low-beamed ceilings, brick-patterned kitchen floor, and Norman Rockwell view overlooking her rolling lawn—and we lifted one another up with stories of kindness. I encouraged the women to notice what was going on around them in the family home, at work, and in the community, and find opportunities to make a positive difference.

The day after Cara hosted that uplifting gathering, she found an opportunity to pay it forward while standing in the checkout line at a craft store. She was in a rush trying to get through her to-do list and in front of her was a young man in a wheelchair. He was having a difficult time making a return and getting his wallet out of his pocket. The women at the checkout counter were getting frustrated as they saw the line back up. As Cara watched this unfold, she said she remembered my mission of *a few kind words* and the power of making our words intentional.

She thought, *I need to protect this man. I need to not be impatient but to be there for him even though I don't know him.* It was the moment to decide to say something kind and change the tone.

She bent down next to the young man and said, "I have a special needs son. If he could do as well as you are right now, I would be so proud of him."

The shy young man blinked back tears and he smiled gratefully at Cara. The women behind the counter watching this beautiful demonstration of kindness in action then softened as well. They in turn encouraged the young man, saying, "You're doing a great job. Take your time."

Later, Cara reflected how "instead of being a situation that could have been explosive, it was a situation where he could leave encouraged and feel a part of society rather than being cast aside. To see the power of kindness through words and patience play out, not just with family and friends but with strangers, was contagious." She made an intentional choice to lift up rather than tear down with her words and actions. It made the checkout clerks' day, and Cara's day, as they watched the young man pull himself up straighter in his chair and wheel himself out of the store with dignity.

Consider This

We rarely know what's going on in someone's life, so always assume they could benefit from your kind thought. We have the power to help and to heal with our words, both written and spoken. Your everyday interactions can provide a host of opportunities for meaningful connection.

For Your Journey

When you're having a bad day, summon the strength to write an unexpected letter of appreciation to someone. I know that can feel like heavy lifting, when life is challenging, but remaining stuck in a difficult place is harder on us. The magic of these letters works both ways: Your energy level will get a positive jolt, and your day just might get better.

Chapter 8

Kindness is a Judgment-free Zone

---

*"Wow, your letter just arrived, and I feel
like an angel of mercy landed on my
shoulder and hugged my heart today. Thank
you so much for your kindness. You made me
feel terrific XOXO."*

—Lynn, letter recipient

PEOPLE OFTEN ASK if I have had any bad expe-
riences or reactions from letter recipients. I
offer a resounding *no*. Although I didn't hear back
from every letter recipient, I can tell you that over
the course of this journey, and over all my years of
being a kindness ambassador in one form or another,
I believe my kindness has been positively received. If
it's offered authentically, it will be received with the
grace with which it was offered. Ask yourself, "Does
my day get better or worse when I'm the recipient of
a kindness?"

Let me put more of your fears to rest. Poor pen-
manship is probably the number one concern that
prospective letter writers voice to me. For all of

you concerned about this, I want to encourage you to start to trust the magic of kindness and consider giving kind written words a try. Remember, your handwriting is uniquely you and adds a layer of personalization that is hard to capture in an email or text. Your recipient will be focused on the letter content, not your penmanship.

For those concerned your letter recipients may think you want something from them, or have some sort of ulterior motive, put those concerns aside too. If you write because you simply want to share and connect, then trust that that is how your letter will be received. You can't control how someone responds, but you *can* be part of a growing community of appreciators who are helping soften the edges of this sometimes hard and judgmental world we share.

Be willing to get a little bit uncomfortable—because the reward is worth the discomfort. The next letter you write will be easier. I have never regretted sharing a kind thought, but I have certainly regretted not sharing one.

The University of Chicago Booth School of Business professor Nicholas Epley, together with University of Texas at Austin McCombs School of Business assistant professor Amit Kumar recently conducted three experiments in which study participants wrote handwritten letters expressing gratitude and then predicted how surprised, happy, or potentially awkward their recipients would feel. Epley and Kumar's results showed that people expressing gratitude *underestimated* how pleasantly surprised recipients would be, and how positive the expression of gratitude made recipients feel. On the flipside, people who wrote letters *overestimated* the potential awkwardness that someone receiving a heartfelt note would experience. The researchers also found that the letter writers were unduly concerned about their ability to express their gratitude skillfully. Although the writers worried about choosing the right words, recipients were happy simply by the warmth of the gesture.[8]

My own journey reinforced that most letter recipients will indeed be happy by the warmth of the gesture. My recipients expressed a feeling of gratitude that I took the time to think about them and share lovely thoughts. I encourage you to trust that your letter recipients will not be judging anything about you. In my estimation, kindness is a judgment-free zone.

Never underestimate the power of your words! Just because you may never hear back from a letter recipient doesn't mean your note was not impactful. If your kindness is expressed with no ulterior motive, then I believe it will be an energizing, positive connection for both parties. It's time to reset your normal and try something new. See how it feels. You can always go back to keeping your kind thoughts to yourself if you don't like it. Or you just might find that you like feeling more energized, empowered, and uplifted when you share.

Lisa and the Reminder in Her Wallet

Tom and I were attending the engagement party for the son of our friends. From across the room, I saw a lovely woman whom I had written one of my notes to at least two months earlier. I hadn't seen or heard from her since writing the note.

Lisa was someone I didn't know well but had always felt a connection to. She's warm and welcoming, and we both found our calling in therapy/coaching later in life. It had been a joy to write to her and let her know I believed she was using her gifts to make this world a better place.

When we finally found our way to each other that evening, she exclaimed, "Your letter overwhelmed me." Then, what she did next humbled me. She took out her wallet and showed me she was now carrying my letter with her every day. She told me it was a reminder to her that she is worthy.

Now it was my turn to feel overwhelmed. When I'd written that letter two months earlier, never could I have imagined it would have the impact it did, and be carried with her everywhere she went. I thought I was just sharing a few kind thoughts. But to my friend, I was validating her and reminding her to shine her light.

Consider This

Kindness is a judgment-free zone. Your letter recipient will not be judging your penmanship or your motive. They'll just be overwhelmed by the warmth of the gesture. Just because you may never hear back from your letter recipient doesn't mean your letter was not impactful.

For Your Journey

Time to get brave and take a risk, no more excuses. Who in your extended life is deserving of an unexpected letter of appreciation? Go find a piece of paper and a pen and take a deep breath. In chapter 10, I will show you how to write one.

Chapter 9

Be The Role Model Our Children Deserve

"When given the choice between being right or being kind, choose kind."

—R. J. Palacio, author of *Wonder*

WHEN I ASKED the large group of fourth graders in my *A Few Kind Words* zoom workshop, "Who said this quote and what book is it from?" there was a wild waving of little hands. I could see many of them rising up out of their seats with enthusiasm, hoping I would call on them.

I called on a little boy who looked like he wanted to absolutely jump through the screen. He said proudly, "Mr. Browne and *Wonder*."

This wonderful group of ten-year-olds were reading the wildly successful and brilliantly written book called *Wonder*. "A powerful story of a 10-year-old boy named Auggie Pullman, who has a facial anomaly," wrote one reviewer. "He is an ordinary kid who plays Xbox, is obsessed with *Star Wars*, but despite the 27 operations done for his face he will never look normal." The book is called *Wonder* because it makes you wonder how you would behave if you were "him" or "them." This amazing book is age appropriate for the entire world. My message of kindness, which is also age appropriate for every person living, worked seamlessly with the theme of kindness in the book.

It just so happened I was speaking with these fourth graders on National Superhero Day. Yes, there is such a day, and it's on April 28th. "The idea behind Superhero Day is a day to honor those who serve and protect while fighting evil. No matter who your favorite hero is, honoring the real or fictional people that inspire us is a worthwhile cause," NationalToday. com explains.

I have always referred to kindness as our super-power, and this lucky coincidence played right into my talk. I let the kids in on a little secret: They have their very own superpower which makes them super-heroes—it's called kindness. I shared another secret with them that their parents, siblings, and teachers had it too, but most of us just don't know how to use this power. You have to practice kindness and make it a part of who you really are, then your power is unleashed!

We talked about my mission and why kindness is a superpower, which is because not only does kind-ness make the person you were kind to feel terrific, but it will make *you* feel terrific every single time you are kind. I told them my hope was that by the end of our time together, each of them would be inspired to tap into their kindness superpower and together we could make this world a better place.

Underneath each of their seats was an invisible superhero cape. I asked them to reach down and put it on with me and imagine in vivid detail what their cape looked like. I described mine as orange with interlocking circles of connection all over the cape and a big K in the middle for kindness. I asked them to wear their cape home and to be sure to wear it back to school the next day and every day they wanted to unleash their kindness superpower.

Hours after my zoom workshop ended, the teachers took fabulous photos of the kids posing as superheroes with their invisible capes on.

Their homework assignment that night was to think about which adult in their lower school community they'd like to write an unexpected letter of appreciation to. The next day they got to write their letters in class using the secret recipe of the three Super S's as a guide:

- Be Sincere
- Keep It Simple
- Be Specific (details in chapter 10).

The teachers told me there was an incredible energy in the classrooms while students wrote their letters of appreciation. When they were told they could deliver their letters, that pent-up energy was released from the classrooms, along with the students, and enveloped the lower school in an invisible high frequency buzz of excitement. The unsuspecting letter recipients were then surprised and delighted to receive their letters.

One letter recipient told one of the fourth grade teachers, "I was in the middle of trying to write a very difficult email to a parent and I was in a bad place. This wonderful letter completely turned my day around." Auggie Pulman in the book, *Wonder*, once said, "I think there should be a rule that everyone in the world should get a standing ovation at least once in their lives." Yes!

> I encourage all of you to put your invisible kindness superhero cape on and give someone the standing ovation they deserve or simply need.

Months later, the head of the lower school told me, "The impact of your work with the children was felt throughout our building and beyond. Our students were moved as they understood the power they each have to make a difference in the world with small gestures of kindness, especially through simple notes and the written word. A couple of the children left me notes over the following weeks/months and each time I received one it made my day, filling me with gratitude for our school community. Several parents reached out to us following the workshop to let us know about notes the children had continued to write at home and how deeply your workshop experience impacted them. During these especially challenging times the power of kindness and helping our children develop empathy is more important than ever."

Just a few months ago, I was able to visit this school in person and spent two days meeting with the third to fifth graders, lower school faculty, and the parents association. Each class participated in an exercise that illustrated for the students and the teachers the impact of *a few kind words*.

I had the teachers sit in the front of the room and I asked each student to take just five minutes and write one anonymous, detailed appreciation for their teacher. They were folded and put into a bowl. Then I read each one out loud. The enormous collective feeling of love and gratitude had every teacher wiping their eyes and the students all brimming with smiles. It was a beautiful demonstration of the power of our words, and it only took a few minutes. This primed them for the second part of the workshop, which was to once again write a letter to any adult in the lower school community. Their enthusiasm for this assignment was palpable and contagious.

Kids love to be part of projects that make their world a better place. Our duty as parents, teachers, mentors, and role models is to teach our kids to feel kindness. Not just talk about kindness. There's a lot of talk about what I call "easy" kindness, like holding the door for someone, but we need to spend time teaching the character building value of "hard" kindness too, such as making the choice to invite a new student to join your lunch table. I believe this is as necessary as feeding, bathing, and clothing our children.

We can't control how others act, but we can control how we act and how we choose to treat one another.

What if each night around the dinner table you shared how you were kind today? What if kindness was a family value that got discussed?

Have you ever written your child or any child an unexpected letter of appreciation? Have your kids seen you write one to someone else?

When I was the director of alumni relations at a school, my favorite day of the year was what we called the "100 Day Ceremony." This was a surprise luncheon for the senior class 100 days before graduation when they'd become alumni.

I had the happy task of asking every parent to write their child an unexpected letter of appreciation that would be distributed at the luncheon. The seniors would excitedly walk into the room, decorated with the school colors and balloon centerpieces, not knowing what was going on. There were always whispered mumblings as they saw the table filled with letters addressed to each of them.

When they took a seat, they were told their parents had written them a letter and they could go find their letter that was alphabetically displayed on the table. As each letter was opened, the room became more still. Each student became completely absorbed by what they were reading. In the unusually hushed silence of an exuberant senior class, I felt both privileged and like an invader to witness this precious connection between parent and child. What will always remain etched in my heart is the image of the big tough guys in the class wiping their eyes. Don't wait for an occasion. The children in your life need to know you love them unconditionally.

Kindness doesn't need to be extraordinary. It should just be a way of life. As ordinary as a peanut butter and jelly sandwich. According to Maurice Elias, Rutgers University psychology professor and author of *Promoting Social and Emotional Learning*, "Kindness can be taught, and it is a defining aspect of civilized human life. It belongs in every home, school, neighborhood, and society."[9]

Bullying is a pervasive problem in our schools and one proven antidote to bullying is kindness. I know this is stripped down and very general, but I wonder if the bully would bully if they had ever been told that they matter? I love this advice from the blog "Inspire Kindness": "Research has shown that 'zero-tolerance' and punishment tactics don't work in the face of bullying. Kindness wins for everyone. When a child is experiencing bullying, it's crucial for them to be able to recall the friend that reached out, the smile from a stranger, and the encouragement from a teacher. Bullies need to be shown kindness, too. They need to have adults and kids in their lives who serve as kindness examples, and they need to be able to recall moments they experienced compassion and understanding."[10]

When you lead with kindness instead of anger, judgment, or impatience, your success rate in whatever it is you are seeking to do will improve. Our children are watching us. They need us to show them the way.

Consider This

Kindness is a superpower that every child and every adult has. Often, they just don't know it. It's our job as adults to model kindness for our children. It's our job to ensure that kindness is taught in schools. It's a key ingredient in the recipe for *thriving*. Our children are watching us.

For Your Journey

Put on your Kindness Superpower Cape and then make sure the children in your life have theirs on, too. What child in your life needs a standing ovation? Consider writing an unexpected letter of appreciation to a deserving child. Remember to be specific. Give them nuggets they can hold on to when times get tough. You'll be helping them believe in themselves.

Chapter 10

How to Write an Unexpected Letter of Appreciation

"I've learned that people will forget what you said, people will forget what you did, but people will never forget how you made them feel."

—Maya Angelou

WHEN WRITING ONE of your own letters of appreciation, in the words of our wonderful son-in-law, "don't overthink it!" You're sharing a kind thought. Not writing a paper. You'll be appreciated, not graded. Remember, your letter recipient will be grateful for the warmth of the gesture. Sharing your kind thoughts unleashes a superpower that will help you feel energized, empowered, and uplifted every time you write an unexpected letter of appreciation.

Here we go.

Surprise Them!

It's the unexpectedness that makes these letters so deliciously memorable. Although it's always nice to write what you appreciate about someone in their birthday or holiday card, it's incredibly impactful to get one of these letters out of the blue with nothing attached to it except pure gratitude. I encourage you to write your letter/s of appreciation when the mood strikes you. Don't wait for an occasion. The surprise adds an extra layer of delectable buttercream frosting to the cake.

Someone You Appreciate

The first step is to find someone you appreciate. Maybe you already have a list of potential recipients you've been creating as you read about my journey. Many of my workshop attendees have shared they're more comfortable writing their first letter to some-one who's not part of their intimate circle. They don't want to get too vulnerable all at once but rather ease into this practice. If that resonates with you, then write to someone you're not very close with but admire, appreciate, or respect.

If no one jumps to mind, then I invite you to spend the next week noticing and paying attention to all those you come in contact with. This starts with your partner at home, your children, your barista, your bus driver, your colleagues, your crossing guard, your mailman, your dry cleaner, your friends, and your acquaintances. We miss opportunities to connect on a regular basis because we've not cultivated a practice of awareness. Be an observer. Look for the gifts each person has instead of their faults. You've entered a judgment-free zone. Sometimes you have to actively engage people to help them shine their light. Ask them questions and remember to listen to their answer. I believe you'll be very pleasantly surprised by what you discover. When you notice a behavior that you appreciate, don't keep it to yourself. It is time to write your letter!

When Writing the Letter...

Remember the recipe of the Three Super S's:
1. **Be Sincere.** Be your wonderful, beautiful, authentic self. Don't waste your time if you're trying to win someone over or get something in return. It'll be obvious if your intentions are fake. Write from the heart. People respond well to someone who is honest, genuine, and willing to get a little vulnerable. All traits that accompany sincerity. When you share sincere thoughts, you're building trust and that feels gratifying for both the writer and the recipient.
2. **Keep It Simple.** Sincerity is more meaningful than length. Get right to the point.

No one needs flowery language. What your recipient needs to know is that they matter, so don't keep them waiting. Let them know why you are writing them a letter in the first few sentences. I wrote on two sides of a folded 4-by-6-inch notecard. You can write on a yellow sticky pad, loose leaf paper, or monogrammed stationery. It can be three sentences or three pages. List your reasons why you appreciate, admire, or respect your recipient, then seal the note with gratitude and mail it or hand deliver it or leave it on your partner's pillow.

3. **Be Specific.** The magic lives in the details. It's wonderful to know that you appreciate someone in general, but to write down why, specifically, you appreciate them is what makes them save that letter, makes the tears start to flow, and makes them feel valued and noticed. You can share one appreciation that's meaningful to you or several appreciations. It's the description of why you admire, respect, love, or appreciate them that will "make their day."

Avoid "Thank You"

In all my letters of appreciation, I have chosen to never use the words "thank you." This is a very deliberate practice because I believe that true appreciation comes from a deep place of feeling.

Thank you can be a societal norm we say sometimes with little meaning attached to it. We are raised to say please and thank you. How often do you hear parents say, "What do you say…?"

That's necessary, great training, and I'm not discouraging it. It's a vitally important part of etiquette in our society, and I hope you'll say it often. But I also think that sometimes it's said by rote.

Appreciation calls for a more intentional response. An appreciation is a feeling of gratitude, whereas a thank you is an expression of gratitude. Verbalizing or putting into writing what we appreciate about someone takes some thought. It means you actively engaged and noticed something above and beyond about someone. I offer you this idea of not using thank you in your letters of appreciation as it makes you get a little more thoughtful in what you write. However, you may feel differently about this idea, and I encourage you to write in the way that feels most natural to you.

Sample Opening/Greeting

1. I had a nice thought about you today and I wanted to share it.
2. You crossed my mind today and I smiled.
3. I can't tell you how much I appreciate your kindness today.
4. When I entered the coffee shop today, I never expected to leave with such a smile on my face.

Sample Content

1. I appreciate the way you run such an efficient and professional meeting.
2. I so appreciate how you always make me and everyone else feel so welcome.
3. I appreciate your warm smile and good humor. You have a contagious energy about you.
4. I appreciate what an engaged listener you are. You always give me your undivided attention, and in this distracted world, I want you to know how much that means to me.

Sample Closing

1. Keep shining your bright light. You're making a difference in this world. With gratitude and appreciation.
2. I'm so glad you're in my life.
3. I will always appreciate your kind and gentle way.

Remember, writing unexpected letters of appreciation takes courage and a willingness to get a little uncomfortable. You're making the proactive choice to put into action your generosity of spirit. There's no downside, and the upside is a kinder you. I believe with all my heart you'll like who you're being when you write unexpected letters of appreciation.

The following are examples of letters from my journey:

Dear Marty,

I was thinking about you today and it's such a shame not to share loving thoughts. So here are my thoughts —

Marty, you always greet me and everyone with such a genuine smile. You make it seem like you are so happy to see me. I can't tell you how much I appreciate that. Your warmth just spills out of you and onto whomever you are with. You are authentic and kind and interested. One word that comes to mind when I think of you is inclusive. You bring people together and are always so welcoming.

I know that you have been through some very difficult times and yet you always appear joyful. You embrace fully whatever you are doing. You have an enormous circle of love around you because of who you are. I am so happy and lucky to share a little slice of that circle. You're a rock star, Marty.

With gratitude and appreciation, Tracey

Dear Brent, Elizabeth, Maya, and Quinn,

There is something truly magical about the way the four of you interact with each other and others. You all are the embodiment of family. You share a beautiful respect for all those in your orbit, you embrace life with vigor and fun, and collectively, your compassionate hearts make this world a better place.

I believe with all my heart that our relationships are the most important things in our lives.

Your family is a role model for how to treat others. You all are active listeners, your faith guides your actions, you make those around you feel heard and noticed, and you love freely and openly. I can't imagine more beautiful traits.

Elizabeth, your hugs are delivered with such authenticity. You're one of the most joyful and self-less people I know. Brent, your smile melts my heart. You care so deeply and meaningfully about all that is important to you. Maya, you are so courageous and confident and smart. I so admire your ability to be true to yourself. Quinn, your sparkle is infectious and contagious. You are so kind and interested in everything. As a family, you open your hearts and home to everyone in need. I have such a smile on my face as I think about how grateful I am to know you all.

Keep shining your bright lights. You really seem to get what's important in this world. You're making a difference every day when you share your positive, kind, and loving energy.

With gratitude and appreciation, Tracey

Be a Kindness Multiplier!

I challenge you to write an unexpected letter of appreciation to a different person every day for just one week and see how you feel. If you want support, then get others involved. This is the type of project that's fun and energizing to do with a group of people. Consider asking your family to join you in this week-long exercise or get your department at work to be part of your challenge. Encourage your book group to get involved.

You x 7 letters = 7 letters

Your family of 4 people x 7 letters = 28 letters

Your book group of 10 people x 7 letters = 70 letters

Your department at work of 15 people x 7 letters = 105 letters

The Exponential Factor

You can exponentially be part of a global kindness movement. The conversation around the dinner table when you share each night who you wrote to is suddenly filled with positive energy. The same thing at work and at book group. Intentional kindness is contagious and shifts the energy around you from negative or neutral to positive every time.

My letter writing journey is just an example of how one person can make a difference. Although I do know that my intentional kindness touched the lives of 365 people, what I'll never know is how many subsequent people's lives were enriched by the pay-it-forward kindness of those 365 people. How many people's lives will you enrich?

Consider This

There are three Super S's to writing an impactful letter of appreciation. No matter who you write to, keep these in mind: Be Sincere, Keep It Simple, and Be Specific. Consider not using the words thank you in your letters. An appreciation is a feeling of gratitude, whereas a thank you is an expression of gratitude.

For Your Journey

I challenge you to write an unexpected letter of appreciation every day for just one week and see how you feel. Eight people will be energized, empowered, and uplifted because you chose to take the time to focus on positivity and notice the good stuff around you. Eight people? Yes, eight. You, the letter writer, need to be included in that count because you'll be just as uplifted as your seven lucky recipients.

Chapter 11

Why Our Words Matter

---

*"I just got your note, and I am in tears.
No one ever speaks to me that way. Thank
you for taking the time to write. It's such a
beautiful, heartfelt note, and I appreciate it
more than you can possibly imagine."*
—Katy, letter recipient

*"I was blown away. I got home from a trip
and went through the pile of mail and
found your letter. I literally cried. No one
has ever done that for me before. I might
actually frame it! I will certainly add it to
my pile of treasures. Thank you so much!"*
—Wendy, letter recipient

THERE ARE SO many lessons and treasures I'll take away from this journey, but the one that touches me deep in my core is that many of my letter recipients said some version of "No one has ever said that to me before." These words came from people who, from my estimation, have it all going on—accomplished professionals, educators, parents, and friends. To think my few kind thoughts were the first time anyone had made them feel seen in this way just hurts my heart. This is very different from "I was having a bad day and got your letter." For these recipients, my letter touched a place of longing that wasn't visible but was soothed by my unexpected words of appreciation.

These kinds of comments have made me believe with every bit of my being that the world needs a movement of *A Few Kind Words*. I want people to believe in their worth every day and I imagine a world where we're not afraid to tell ourselves, our peers, our children, our bosses, our colleagues, and our neighbors we all deserve to be here. For although it may look to the outside world that we are confident and don't need validation, my journey has proven otherwise.

Every single one of us can benefit from being told regularly that we deserve to be here. When our gifts are acknowledged we stand a little taller and a little more sure of ourselves.

Our words have an incredible energy behind them. They can lift up, inspire, and transform or they can deflate and crush. If you rearrange the letters in "words" you get "sword," a perfect illustration of the power our words can yield to cut us to the quick or send us soaring to beautiful heights. The words you use *matter*. When you speak or write words of kindness, a high frequency energy is released that wraps around you and your recipient, bringing you into the present moment and allowing you to connect on a higher level. The more you practice kindness to yourself and others, the more you will live surrounded by this higher, nourishing energy.

Think about how much more room there would be in our hearts, minds, bodies, and souls if hate and judgment were removed. We'd all have so much more space ready to give and receive affirmations and appreciations. It's very possible to boost someone's confidence and defuse anger, violence, and hatred—just tell them that they matter. Assume everyone you have a connection with has an invisible longing to be seen. You're powerful beyond measure. Don't waste it. I don't want anyone to ever say again "no one has ever said that to me before."

T and Our Universal Need

I have known T for a few decades. We are social friends more than intimate friends. We have kids of similar ages, lots of mutual friends, and I have had the pleasure of volunteering with her. I have the utmost respect for her professionally as well as personally. Also, she always makes me laugh.

The trait I have admired most about T is her ease with people. She's an active listener and possesses a thoughtful and calm communication style. She's warm, gentle, and kind. I wrote an unexpected letter of appreciation to her after being in a meeting together and watching her shine. A few weeks later I received a handwritten note from her followed by a phone call.

What she shared has stayed with me for the past few years: "I've been in therapy for years trying to become the person you told me I already am." She shared that she struggles so much to feel calm and present with people. She has been working on anxiety and self-hate and how to let her light shine. Receiving my letter out of the blue "was a mind blower!" she wrote. "But so confirming that what I hope, what I intend to give others is possible. So, thank you Tracey for your gift."

All I had hoped when I put pen to paper was that the smile that had naturally spread across my face while writing to my friend would be transposed to her face upon reading my letter. I had no idea she was doubtful about her many gifts that were so apparent to me. I'm so grateful I took the time to write to T. Her response reinforced for me the absolutely universal need we all have to be acknowledged. It's why I write these letters. If left to our own devices, we often forget about the attributes that make us special. Having people in your life remind you from time to time of your awesomeness can go a long way.

Kindness and Mental Health Are Deeply Connected

In 2020, we found that 63% of UK adults agree that when other people are kind it has a positive impact on their mental health, and the same proportion agree that being kind to others has a positive impact on their mental health.

Showing kindness to others
- is an antidote to isolation;
- creates a sense of belonging;
- helps reduce stress;
- brings a fresh perspective;
- deepens friendships.

Being kind to ourselves
- prevents shame from corroding our sense of identity;
- helps boost self-esteem;
- improves feelings of confidence and optimism.[11]

Consider This

Just because someone appears to the outside world as confident and not in need of our appreciation is no reason not to share your kind thoughts. Your words may touch a place of longing in a way you never could have imagined.

For Your Journey

Who do you know who may be struggling with something right now? Who could benefit from finding an uplifting surprise in their mailbox? Often when we are not in a good place we go inward when what we really need is our community. Be that community for someone and remind them of their special attributes. Let them know you see them and are walking with them on their journey.

Chapter 12

Linger Mindfully

"Last evening, I sat and read your letter. I can't tell you how much I enjoyed reading it. It's a special person who takes the time to send a thoughtful note, for no other reason but to share. Too often we move through our day consumed by our 'to do lists' and lost in our internal thoughts. You've reminded me of the importance of the 'pause' and 'sharing' for no other reason but to acknowledge another person. Thank you for your thoughtfulness—it was so unnecessary, but I read the letter three times, nonetheless!!"

—Peter, letter recipient

MERRIAM-WEBSTER DESCRIBES THE word "linger" as *to be slow in parting or in quitting something*. I've come to love this action verb, and at the end of my letter writing journey, I was surprised to find I had what I now call a lingering lifestyle.

Lingering is what helped me find my 365 letter

recipients. It's what allowed me to notice what I was missing. All those wonderful interactions that led to meaningful connections.

Lingering drew me into the present moment and helped me understand what living mindfully really means. For me, it's noticing the sounds, smells, and tastes of life in a way I glossed over before. Textures became more three dimensional, colors became more vivid, aromas caught my attention, and people became more interesting. When I lingered instead of rushed, I was replenished.

Mindfulness carried over to the act of writing my letters. The slow intentionality of this practice was restorative, rejuvenating, and at times even healing. Somehow, putting pen to paper made me more thoughtful about my word choice. I discovered that to write an authentic letter of appreciation, I needed to be fully present. It's simply impossible to be authentic and, at the same time, distracted by a to-do list in your head. I would collect my stationery, a stamp, and my favorite blue pen. When I sat down at my kitchen counter, took a deep breath, and visualized who I was writing to, I could feel myself slowly becoming fully present and calmer. I would fill my mind with the positive traits of my person of the day and begin to write. The calm feeling lingered long after the envelope was sealed and mailed.

Kindness mixed with mindfulness is a medicine for which you don't need insurance. It's a form of universal healthcare that's overlooked and underused. Every person on Earth can take this medicine for free and benefit from it, because on a purely physical level, regular doses of kindness

- release the feel-good hormone serotonin and raise endorphin levels, giving you a "helpers high";
- reduce anxiety;
- reduce inflammation and thereby alleviate pain;
- reduce stress;
- release oxytocin, which reduces blood pressure, benefiting the heart;
- boost the immune system.[12]

Wouldn't it be amazing if instead of continuing to see a rise in addictions to opioids and sugar, we became addicted to the rush of the feel-good hormones dopamine, oxytocin, and serotonin that are released whenever we practice kindness? Humankind is yearning for us to strive to be our best selves now more than ever. The judgmental, self-centered, ego-driven way just hasn't been working. I don't understand at what point in life's history our default system became one of fear and lack, but I am choosing to see the glass as half full and I invite you to join me and linger for a little while. It feels so much better.

Consider This

Linger is an action verb. Lingering allowed me to notice what I was missing, all those wonderful interactions that led to meaningful connections. When you linger mindfully and engage in the world around you, you may find that you do indeed have *a few kind words* to share. Then, enjoy all the physical benefits that will wash over you when you practice intentional kindness regularly.

For Your Journey

Where in your life could you linger more? No relationship has ever improved by dashing off. Next time you're inclined to rush out of a meeting to get to the next thing on your to-do list, linger instead. It doesn't have to be for long. Engage one person in conversation of a personal nature. People love to talk about their families, their pet projects, their pets, their hobbies, or their vacation plans. Please don't play the I'm too busy card. No one is ever too busy to care. You'll still get everything done, because you always do, but I bet you will feel lighter for having flexed your kindness and lingering muscles.

Chapter 13

"Who Has Loved You into Being?"

"There are three ways to ultimate success:
The first way is to be kind. The second way
is to be kind. The third way is to be kind."

—Mr. Rogers

"WHO AS LOVED you into being?" Mr. Rogers asked that magnificently intro-spective question when he was receiving a Lifetime Achievement Award. I invite you to let this settle into your bones and let your mind wander for an answer.

Think back to the people who encouraged you, supported you, listened to you, and role-modeled a value system that has carried you to where you are today. Has anyone made you feel cherished? That beautiful word means to "hold dear and protect and care for lovingly." None of us have become the people we are today by ourselves.

Who's that person you can't wait to tell when something happens to you, whether fabulous or mundane? Who's that person you can squish together on the couch with and watch, on a shared cell phone screen, endless funny videos of people getting scared that make you laugh so hard no sound comes out? Who do you instantly call when your heart is shattered, and who do you want to hug tightly and share in your joy when you get that promotion or finally create that piece of art that's been inside you for so long?

Think about the people who've loved you into being, then find a quiet time, close your eyes, and let your mind fill with images of that person. Use your five senses. Breathe in the scent of their perfume or shampoo, picture what they're wearing, listen for their laughter or their calming words of advice and support, conjure up the taste of a shared meal or a lingering kiss, and feel their arms around you in a safe and enduring hug.

A white buttercream birthday cake with hot pink flowers and strawberry filling will forever be synonymous with our mother's love for Wendy and me. I close my eyes now and I can see her slicing for me, the birthday girl, the first piece of cake with the biggest pink flower on top as I swipe my finger across the frosting and taste the sweetness of both the buttercream and Mom's love.

My husband and his three siblings all equate their mother's love with the sound of her jingling charm bracelet when she would quietly come into their bedrooms after a night out and kiss their sleepy faces goodnight. It's a privilege to witness someone being loved into being, and that's what I get to experience watching our daughter-in-law, Jenna, shower our grandsons, Hudson and Maverick, with enduring patience and absolute respect every day making them feel safe and loved unconditionally.

Who are you imagining? Most likely, these people already know you love and appreciate them, but that's no reason not to put your gratitude into writing. To express your gratitude in writing using specific details why this person or people have helped you become your best self is a gift that keeps on giving.

To validate the existence of another human being is one of the most beautiful and selfless gifts we can give. In doing so, we also validate ourselves.

We thrive when we are in community. Acknowledging the positive attributes we each have and the impact we have on one another is immeasurable. So often we assume someone knows how we feel about them. I am asking you to never assume. Tell them. If they already know or if they don't know, either way, reading your words of appreciation will strengthen your bonds in the most beautiful way.

Dianne, We're In This Together!

"I can't tell you how meaningful it was to get your note. It was the most thoughtful heartwarming note imaginable and literally warmed my entire being to the core. Thank you for the incredibly generous gift of those words, and of your sacred friendship. I love you so much!"

I was in the ladies clothing department of Target looking for elastic-waisted pants for my mother. Since she broke her hip and had become much frailer, she could no longer maneuver buttons and zippers. The aides in her skilled nursing unit told me as soon as I arrived from my traffic-filled journey that I needed to get her new pants today. I googled the closest Target and promised Mom I would be back as soon as I could.

All I could find were sweatpants with Adidas in large print down the leg, or a purple velour sweat-suit, neither of which were my conservative mother's style. Then my phone rang. I answered, so relieved it was not Mom's skilled nursing department calling, but my dearest friend, Dianne. She was calling to tell me she had just opened her mail and had read a letter from me that touched her heart. I could tell from the shaking in her voice she had tears in her eyes as she said over and over that my letter would be residing forever in the polished wooden box on the dining room shelf that held her most special possessions.

Dianne and I have been best friends since 1985, in Boston, when Tom introduced us. I was working for Procter and Gamble and Dianne and Tom were working on the same team at Xerox. We literally became best friends after one dinner. I've never experienced such an instant and visceral connection. Pre-children, we spent hours antiquing, decorating, smothering our dogs with love, and doing what best friends do, talking endlessly about absolutely every-thing and nothing. We weren't big on silence and still aren't. There is simply too much to discuss whenever we're together. We both feel things deeply, like our souls are connected and we have the identical sense of humor. The best laughing attack of my life happened when Tom called to tell me he drank Dianne's contact lenses by mistake when they were on a work trip.

We embrace our similarities and our differences, loving each other completely as we are. Way back before it was a "thing," Dianne would scrub all her fruits and veggies with soap and water. I would pass my fruits and veggies under the faucet once and call them washed. I didn't tell Dianne she was insane when she hand-painted every third flower blue on her family room drapes because her favorite color was missing from the fabric design. And she didn't call me obsessed when I would buy anything with a white cat on it because it reminded me of my first love, Marty, my cat.

We've been there for every major and minor event in each other's lives. We were pregnant at the same time and talked every day about the strange and miraculous things that were happening to our bodies. We were at each other's hospital bedside when our babies were just hours old. We started a furniture painting business together called "Edelweiss," collected Christmas ornaments together, and took endless photographs of our families because every moment was memorable.

The friendship remained just as deep and indestructible when Tom and I moved to New Jersey in 1993. We made emergency trips to a hotel halfway between Massachusetts and New Jersey when one of us was in need or we just needed a touch point. Our families spent countless New Year's Eves together on New England ski trips and created precious memories on trips to a lake in Vermont and the beach on Cape Cod. Dianne is the first person I had the courage to whisper to, decades ago, that someday I would like to write a book.

I have absolute certainty that Dianne knows I would move heaven and Earth for our friendship. Yet, I still wrote her *a few kind words* because even when we know we are loved, seeing the words in writing still stops us in our tracks, as Dianne reaffirmed with her phone call. My life is more complete because of this friendship, and I never want to take for granted that Dianne, or anyone important to me, knows this. I want to tell them my world is better because they're in it.

While I was writing this note, I could feel my whole body filling with warmth. There was a physical release of endorphins when I was thinking about the love and endless support Dianne and I share, and the unshakable trust earned over decades of showing up for each other. We've always said "we're in this together." No matter what "this" is. Writing this note was a joyful experience that sustained me for days. Little did I know it would sustain me again, days later, during a stressful moment in Target.

Standing between the clothing racks filled with pants my sweet mother would never like, I found myself crying into the phone right along with my bestie. Dianne told me she was overwhelmed by my words and so deeply grateful that I took the time to write the note. We reaffirmed our love, appreciation, and affirmation for one another, all because I put in writing what we both already knew. My note allowed us both to be unexpectedly lifted up. It allowed us to pause, and it allowed our present moment to get exponentially better. For me, I got a temporary reprieve from my endless worry about Mom and a nourishing laughing attack as we envisioned my mother in a purple velour sweatsuit. Dianne, rushing between meetings, found a cherished gift among the bills when she checked her mail. She slowed down and she felt loved.

My letter to Dianne:

———

Dear Dianne,

Your friendship just makes my heart sing! I was just thinking about you today and decided to share it with you. I value so much about you—who you are and how you conduct yourself in this world. You are a bright light, my sweet friend, and I am so grateful that you are in my life.

Dianne, your care and love for those who are important to you is beautiful to see. You are an active listener, and your warmth just spills out of you onto whomever you are connecting with. Our long and deep conversations touch my soul and nurture me. Finding someone who you can be totally authentic with is a gift... You are my gift.

Our shared history filled with beautiful and difficult memories is part of the fabric of our lives.

I cherish all those memories and look forward to decades more. You are kind and smart and creative and professional and loving. You, Dianne, radiate compassion, and empathy and define for me what friendship means. I love you.

With gratitude and appreciation, Tracey

Consider This

Who has loved you into being? None of us have gotten where we are today by ourselves. We thrive when we're in community. Please don't ever assume your loved ones know how you feel. Tell them often and maybe your letter will find its way into someone's box of treasures.

For Your Journey

Which of the people who've loved you into being is getting an unexpected letter of appreciation from you today? Use your five senses and inhale all that makes this person important to you and then exhale it all into your letter.

Chapter 14

Cultivate a Culture of Appreciation at Work

"Ever since hosting your workshop about the importance of sharing A Few Kind Words, I've made a deliberate practice of writing notes to my clients and referral sources. I've always been an advocate of the thank you note, but just sharing what I appreciate, for no specific reason, is something new to my business practice. It's added a new layer of connection."

—Tom, workshop host

WRITING UNEXPECTED LETTERS of appreciation isn't limited to your personal life. The positive ramifications are significant in the workplace. Simply put, appreciation matters.

Lack of appreciation has a hefty price tag attached to it. CNBC's Workforce Wire reports "This is not just an HR issue but a bottom line one as well: business units with engaged workers have 23% higher profit, while employees who are not engaged cost the world $7.8 trillion in lost productivity, equal to 11% of global GDP."[13] Lack of appreciation is one of the main reasons people leave their jobs.

Does your company foster a culture of appreciation? Your company's culture is one of its most powerful assets. Kindness is a morale booster. When you integrate kindness and appreciation into the fabric of your daily work environment, you're laying the groundwork for an inspired, creative, productive, and inclusive work force.

Often people go through their days hearing complaints instead of appreciations. Or worse, they hear nothing and feel invisible. Imagine if, instead, at work it was commonplace to receive unexpected notes of appreciation. A colleague, boss, employee, or client noticed something you did well, and they told you. You didn't have to wait until your yearly review, but you found a note on your desk from someone you work with who took the time to jot down they really enjoy working with you because (fill in the blank.) Motivation and collaboration in the workplace would improve.

As in all relationships, you must build trust to grow a relationship. One of the most powerful ways to grow trust is to actively become aware of the contributions each person brings and then lift each other up with acknowledgment of those contributions. The acknowledgment can be left on a yellow sticky note or on company letterhead. The fact that you took the time to observe and share your appreciation is where the power lies.

One study found that teams in a respectful, kind environment

- possess 26% more energy;
- are 30% more likely to feel motivated and enthusiastic about acquiring new skills and being exposed to new ideas;
- express 36% more satisfaction with their jobs and are 44% more committed to their organizations.[14]

I've given my *A Few Kind Words* workshop at professional organizations from Merrill Lynch to nonprofits. My simple message is always the same: Share your kind thoughts and people will respond in a positive way. What I hear too often from workshop attendees is that although kindness is present in the form of polite behavior, it's routinely not encouraged, or role-modeled as an action step necessary to grow your business.

I'm asking you to become a kindness ambassador for your organization.

Learn about those around you by engaging in meaningful conversations. Ask how you can help. Offer to be a mentor to a new colleague. Find out what organization your client volunteers with and ask them about it. Notice what your assistant, boss, colleague, security guard likes to drink in the morning and surprise them with one just the way they like it.

Consider holding an office retreat called "Everything But Work: Get to Know Each Other!"

Discover fun facts about each employee. Everyone shares their favorite hobbies, music, food, best vacation, bucket list vacation, etc. Future conversations around the water cooler can be so much richer and engaging when you've discovered commonalities.

It takes work to build both professional and personal relationships. As Benjamin Franklin said, "Well done is better than well said." Roll up your sleeves and get to really know one another. No matter what your position in your company, be a role model of intentional kindness. Chances are someone will notice. It feels energizing to be in a work environment where collaboration is the norm and not the exception. I can't imagine time better spent than investing in a culture of appreciation.

Kindness and positivity are core values in the mission statements of more and more organizations. One of my favorites is the clothing company Life is Good. Their mission statement is *to spread the power of optimism*. When asked "Why optimism?" the response is "Every morning, we each wake up with a choice: to focus on the obstacles in our lives, or to focus on the opportunities. Optimism isn't irrational cheerfulness, and it's not blind positivity. It's a powerful approach to accomplishing goals and living a fulfilling life." Their branding and their mission statement are compelling to me. I want to support a company that filters all their decisions through a mission statement like this.

I've had a Life Is Good sticker on my last two cars for the past sixteen years. It's the only sticker I want there. When I was deciding what I'd like to give my workshop attendees as a little takeaway, I knew what it had to be: a Life is Good sticker. When I called the company to place an order, I shared with the sales rep what I wanted them for. He said he loved my mission to let people everywhere know they matter, and he gave me my order for free in the spirit of collaboration. Just as we want to work for organizations who actively recognize the importance of creating and maintaining a culture of appreciation, look for companies that lead with a value system that speaks to you and give them your support.

For all of you leaders and future leaders, consider how intentional kindness can play a role in every decision and interaction you will have. According to Simon Sinek, inspirational speaker and author of *Start with Why: How Great Leaders Inspire Everyone to Take Action*: "Leadership is not about being in charge. Leadership is about taking care of those in your charge."[15]

Consider This

Lack of appreciation is one of the top reasons people leave their jobs. Does your company foster a culture of appreciation? When kindness, respect, and appreciation are demonstrated regularly in the workplace, collaboration and productivity improve.

For Your Journey

I challenge you to add something new to your business practice: Write a note to a client or colleague and share something you admire or appreciate about them. It's not a thank you for their business or support, but an appreciation for the way they conduct themselves or an appreciation for their value system or how they spend their free time. It's affirming and powerful when you notice and acknowledge what's important to someone in and outside of business. This is a meaningful way to take your relationship to the next level. People want to do business with people who make them feel noticed and valued.

Chapter 15

Kindness is My Happily Ever After!

*"Be kind whenever possible. It is always
possible."*

—H.H. the Dalai Lama

M Y ABSOLUTE FAVORITE thing in life is hearing,
watching, or reading happily-ever-after sto-
ries. My Pollyanna mind thrives on hearing about
happy endings. That's why I love kindness so much.
Kindness *always* has a happy ending!

My friends know which books and movies to rec-
ommend to me. They all know I want the happily ever
after. Maybe it's living with blinders on, but maybe
it's choosing to fill my mind and body with the power
of positivity. Kindness is what helps keep negativity
at bay for me. It's not a passive activity but an active
one. It involves making a choice. The choice may not
always be the easy one, but it's always an available one.
It might involve taking some valuable time you didn't
budget for in your day. It might make you uncom-
fortable, at least in the beginning. But, if you decide
to choose the compassionate, generous, caring, and

kind option, you stand a much better chance of living happily ever after. Remember, we're happiest when we connect and are in relationship with one another. Sappy commercials and feel-good movies are always about people feeling loved and noticed. Just like the power you feel when writing or receiving *a few kind words*.

Our oldest child and only son, Ren, was born just five hours before my twenty-seventh birthday. We share a zodiac sign, a penchant for laughing attacks, a super-sensitive heart, and an ease with people. He's charismatic and compassionate, and we're connected on a cellular and cosmic level. Ren just makes me happy. He has since the moment he arrived and gave me the greatest gift, becoming a mom.

Ren has been the recipient of countless "just because" letters from me over his lifetime and I have a treasure trove of unexpected letters of appreciation from him. The most special is the one I keep in our safe deposit box. It's the one he wrote the summer after graduating from high school, when he was a staffman at a camp in Vermont before heading to college. He wrote on three pages ripped out of a spiral notebook telling me in detail how much and why he loved me. Ren had just turned eighteen and even though he was preoccupied with girls, partying, college, and freedom, he took the time to think about his mom and write something precious enough to be stored safely next to our marriage certificate and the deed to our home. Ren is a master wordsmith, and he has continued to share *a few kind words* with people in his world. Now, he is role modeling this for his children.

Trent, the Sanitation Worker

Ren and our then two-and-a-half-year-old grandson Hudson had a wonderful exchange with their sanitation worker, Trent, out in Portland, Oregon. Thursday morning is garbage day and definitely Hudson's favorite day of the week. He's obsessed with big trucks and tractors, and every Thursday he gets to see a recycling truck, a street cleaner, and a garbage truck. Big happenings for a toddler.

The rumble of the truck with the squeaky brakes coming down the street wakes Hudson up and he immediately begins calling for Dada. Ren scoops him up out of his crib and they rush to the front picture window overlooking the street. Hudson frantically waves first to the recycling truck, then to the street sweeper and then to the garbage truck. Week after week the first two trucks never acknowledged the little tow-headed, pajama-clad boy in the window, and every week the sanitation worker always waved back, to Hudson's absolute delight. One day after they waved to each other, the sanitation worker got out of his truck and left something small on top of their garbage can. He smiled at Hudson, got back in his truck, and drove on down the street. Ren and Hudson ran outside and found a metal toy green and white garbage truck, just like the real one.

Hudson flew back inside to show Mama his new

treasure and Ren went to his desk to find a piece of paper and a pen. With Hudson sitting on his lap, Ren explained that they needed to let the nice man know how much they appreciated the little truck. More importantly, they needed to let him know how much they appreciated the extra few seconds he took to acknowledge a little boy in the window each week. Ren wanted to share with this man that not just Hudson but also Mama and Dada were lifted up by this silent relationship that had developed between a stranger and a little boy. Ren realized he didn't even know the driver's name, but he understood the value of kindness and that's what he wrote about. He included a gift card to his favorite sandwich shop and sealed the letter.

He told Hudson that next Thursday they would wait for the kind sanitation worker at the end of the driveway and make a proper introduction. Next week, with Hudson clutching the letter in one little hand and a green and white metal toy truck in his other, they waited at the end of the driveway to hear the rumble of the truck and the squeak of the brakes. When the truck came into sight Hudson started waving. The truck stopped at their driveway and the kind man got out. With a little prodding, Hudson handed the man the white envelope and Ren introduced himself and Hudson.

"I'm Trent," the man said as he looked Hudson right in the eyes. Ren told Trent that he made their day with his simple wave each week and then the gift of the toy truck. He described for Trent the happy

Thursday routine that had developed around his arrival and the joy he has brought them. As Trent climbed back in his green and white truck with the letter clutched in his big hand, he looked down at Hudson and with a wave said, "Hudson makes my day every Thursday." And they all lived happily ever after.

Consider This

Kindness involves making a choice. The choice may not always be the easy one, but it's always an available one. If you choose to be compassionate, generous, caring, and kind you stand a much better chance of living happily ever after.

For Your Journey

Think about your daily and weekly activities. Is there someone, like Trent, who you see all the time but haven't taken the time to get to know? Or maybe you do know them and appreciate them but have never told them? Who could you surprise with an unexpected letter of appreciation?

Chapter 16

Get Creative

"I was so touched by your note to me. It really made my day, and I can't thank you enough. I love the idea of taking the time to appreciate the people you care about. It is the most important thing that we can do with our time."

—Bill, letter recipient

I T WAS EIGHT months and fifteen days into my letter writing journey and letter number 268 was in the mailbox. That night I found a three-page handwritten letter addressed to me on my pillow. When I opened it, I began to cry after reading only the salutation: "Dear Buzz." Tom had written a letter to my adored father, Buzz, who, as you know, had passed away four weeks after we became engaged decades ago. Finding that letter was so unexpected I could feel my chest tightening and my breath getting stuck in my throat as I clearly saw in my mind the two most important men in my life connecting. Tom was sharing with Dad what he considered to be the positive attributes about me that he knew my dad would want to know and be proud of. Tom was very generous with his words and thanked Dad for fathering me, guiding me, and allowing me to be the keeper of his mantra *a few kind words*. He told Dad about our children and how relationships are everything to me.

One of the blessings of my life is that Tom and Dad got to know each other before Dad passed away. I couldn't bear it if they hadn't had the opportunity to laugh together, drink a Michelob together, and share their love of tennis. Dad knew I had found my Corn Flakes Guy, and this has sustained me all these years. Tom has always understood the place in my heart that is reserved solely for Dad, and he has consistently had the utmost respect for the memories I love to share. Over the eight months of my letter writing journey, Tom had been everything a supportive partner should be: encouraging, loving, and a proud sharer of my mission. He tells anyone who will listen about how I am trying to make this world a better place. Since we started dating in Boston, sharing daiquiris on the Boston Esplanade while listening to The Boston Pops free Sunday concert, Tom has lifted me up with his humor and his absolute devotion to me and our family. He is my champion and I like to think I am his. He knows I love surprises, and thirty-three years into our marriage, he found yet another way to win my heart over.

Writing an unexpected letter of appreciation to my father was one of the most endearing, kind, and loving things he has done. He wrote in his informal way that sounds just like he speaks. Tom made me feel cherished because he noticed what's important to me—letter writing and my dad. He got creative and instead of telling me what he appreciates about me, he told Dad. After wiping the tears away, I couldn't stop smiling at the image in my mind of the two men in my life who love me unconditionally catching up with each other in an easy conversational way. This letter has been added to my collection of treasured keepsakes in the shoe box under my dresser.

Tom has adopted *A Few Kind Words* into his life, and I often find him writing unexpected letters of appreciation to his clients and his friends. We both share a love of connecting on a meaningful level. Tom is my everything. He's my gift who keeps on giving.

A Friend and Her New Tradition

I have a friend whose husband passed away unexpectedly several years ago. She and her two adult children wanted to start an annual tradition to remember and honor their husband/father. They were struggling to come up with something that felt nourishing and sustaining to all three of them. A mutual friend had recently hosted my *A Few Kind Words* workshop and she shared with our friend what she learned about the power of writing unexpected letters of appreciation. My friend and her children settled on the idea of each selecting someone close to their husband/father on the anniversary of his passing, and through the written word, sharing stories and moments in time that they remember about him and their letter recipient. Before mailing their unexpected letters of appreciation, the three of them each read aloud their letter to the other two so they can all feel the love and remember together the attributes their husband/father had to offer the world. Their recipients have been surprised and filled with gratitude for the unexpected reconnection to their departed friend, and my friend and her children now have a beautiful tradition of sharing *A Few Kind Words* each year.

Consider This

There are unlimited possibilities for how you can incorporate *A Few Kind Words* into your life. Don't let the abundance of technology stop you from putting pen to paper and thoughtfully and mindfully creating a keepsake in the form of a letter. Maybe even consider starting a tradition around sharing your kind thoughts like my friend and her children have done. Our words can transcend time and space and nestle right into our hearts for eternity.

For Your Journey

Think outside of the box, get creative, and surprise someone in your tribe. Consider these ideas:

- Write your child a yearly letter detailing all their accomplishments, difficulties, fashion trends, habits, and what makes them so unconditionally precious to you. Surprise your child with breakfast out or a picnic lunch, just the two of you, and read them your letter.

- Gather your best friends together for lunch and tuck inside the rolled-up napkin an unexpected letter of appreciation for each friend.

- Pick a bouquet of flowers from your garden or cut some greenery from your yard and tie it together with a bow. Write a feel-good letter for a stranger filled with inspiring words of encouragement and reminders that they are enough. Address the envelope to "Whomever finds this." Leave the bouquet and the letter on a park bench or in the crook of a tree on your favorite walk and make a stranger's day.

Chapter 17

Where Should Kindness Begin?

"My first reaction on reading your note was that you had overestimated me. But on reflection, I see that it's not about how I see myself but how others do. And that it's likely that we are rather hard on ourselves."

—Olive, letter recipient

B EFORE READING ON, answer this question, "Where should kindness begin?" If you answered... *yourself*... then, congratulations, you are right! Jay Shetty, author of *8 Rules of Love*, says, "When we learn to appreciate ourselves, we're never really alone—we're always with someone we love."[16]

What a brilliant and beautiful concept, but why is it so hard? If you're anything like me, then there are plenty of times when you beat yourself up, criticize yourself, and talk to yourself in a way I hope you'd never talk to another human being. Why are we so hard on ourselves? An overarching theme throughout this book is the power of connection. I've shared stories of connection I experienced when I reached out to my community. What I want to talk about in this chapter is how my journey connected me to myself and how kind words both from others and to myself gave me the confidence and permission to invite my dream of writing a book to come alive. Your relationships and your dreams can thrive when you practice this.

Terry Real, relationship therapist, speaker, and author in an interview with Stacey Lindsay, said: "When I talk about connection, the first order of business is creating a connection to yourself in a loving way. How to hold yourself warmly and tenderly in the face of your human imperfections. That's in short supply in this culture."[17]

For about thirty years I've said to myself, and a few select trusted family and friends, that I'd love to write a book someday. The problem was I had no topic in mind, I rarely write and, until recently, I was a complete failure at goal-setting. When I was in my mid-thirties, I had a vision that I hadn't yet done what I was put on this earth to do. I had a strong sensation there was something meaningful and fulfilling in my future, but what it was remained unclear. This was an encouraging and hopeful feeling for the next few decades, but I would be turning sixty soon and I was still searching for my elusive purpose. Is there an expiration date on *purpose*? Would I soon begin to ferment, sour, and be dumped down the proverbial drain? Had I missed my opportunity to write my book and leave a legacy of love for my family and, perhaps, a larger audience?

I've had the same tape running in my head for three decades: "Who're you kidding, you could never write a book. You're not talented enough and you don't have anything worthy to say." It's inconceivable for me to imagine saying to a friend or our children, "You're not talented enough; you have nothing worthy to say. You could never write a book!" I am laughing out loud at the sheer absurdity of doing that. Yet, I felt comfortable saying some form of those defeating sentences to myself for three decades.

The Wolf You Feed

In a beautiful Native American parable, an old grandfather tells his grandson that he feels as if he has two wolves fighting in his heart. The first is the angry, vengeful wolf and the other is the kind, compassionate wolf. When his grandson asks which wolf wins the fight, the grandfather says, "the one that I feed."

Which wolf are you feeding in your heart? Remember, you always have a choice about how you talk to yourself. I am asking you to bet on yourself for a while and see how that feels.

> **Every time you have a negative thought about yourself, try and substitute it with a positive thought. Something that is supportive and validating, just like you would say to your friend. If you want others to believe in your brilliance, then you have to start believing it first.**

An Awareness Exercise

The most important relationship you have is with yourself, and I encourage you to put time and attention into this relationship. I want you to get curious about how you talk to yourself and treat yourself. There are no right or wrong answers.

List all the ways you were kind to yourself this week. Now list all the ways you were unkind to yourself.

Which list was easier for you to answer? If the kind list was easier, then I'm giving you a standing ovation. If the unkind list was easier, that's OK. You're not alone. I hope this exercise will serve as an *aha!* moment for you. I want to offer you the idea that it's not selfish to be kind to yourself, because when you are, it becomes easier for you to then be kind to others. You are deserving of the same kind of love and respect that you give in abundance to those in your orbit.

- Start your day with some deep breaths and a few quiet minutes of mindfulness.
- Enjoy a walk with your dog or your partner on the beach or your favorite wooded path.
- Exercise or read or garden or cook a special meal.
- Soak in a bath or binge watch your most decadent show.
- Have a delicious chat with your bestie.
- Cut yourself some slack when you lose the deal or burn the dinner.

Ask yourself, "What feels nourishing for me?" and then make time for it. When we cut ourselves slack, it becomes easier to cut others some slack. When we treat ourselves with compassion and respect, we start to treat others in our lives with more compassion and respect too.

The thirteenth letter I wrote on my journey was to myself. I jumped right into my uncomfortable zone and tried something new. This was hard and I had a natural resistance to writing to myself but I allowed myself the time and the courage to consider what I appreciate about myself and then put the words on paper. Seeing it in writing somehow made them more believable. This exercise helped me realize that when you become your own advocate, goals and dreams seem more achievable. Just like the character in your favorite book grows and evolves, so can we evolve. If you tell yourself something long enough, you just might start believing it. You may have done that already with the negative self-talk. It works just the same way with positive self-talk. What we focus on expands so we might as well choose to get comfortable with focusing on what empowers us. Don't let the angry, vengeful wolf win. Feeding the kind, compassionate wolf feels so much better.

One of my coaching clients has instituted a wonderful self-care practice into her life. She collects cards with inspiring sayings on the front. When she's having an empowering day, she fills a card with words of appreciation about herself. She seals it and puts it away until it's needed. When she's having a self-doubt day, she opens the drawer and treats herself to a dose of self-love as she reads her own words reminding herself of her worth.

Over the course of my twelve-month letter writing journey, I received the most validating, supportive, and kind responses to my letters. Many recipients suggested I should write a book about my journey. I thought, "Maybe I finally do have a topic for a book. Maybe I do have a message worthy of sharing with the world. Maybe that story I've been telling myself for the past thirty years was just a placeholder until kindness could finally push fear out of the way."

Fun fact: Fear has an expiration date. It was my fear that was fermenting, souring, and needed to be poured down the drain. Purpose has no expiration date!

I had no idea how liberating it would feel to let kindness sit in the driver's seat of my mind and relegate fear to the back seat. Sometimes I look in the rearview mirror and wave to my old companion fear, just to make sure he's safely belted in and can't climb into the front seat with me again. This self-imposed journey just kept presenting me with unexpected nuggets of delight as my outward kindness kept being reflected onto me and connecting me to the best parts of myself. Receiving beautiful responses allowed fear to shrink, courage and confidence to grow, and ultimately led to writing this book.

I continued to visualize the successful completion of this book, and these visualizations became my daily companions. They were *a few kind words* to myself and my encouragement not to give up when I started to doubt myself again. The kind words I was now able to say allowed me to throw off the armor I had so meticulously worn and polished, supposedly protecting me from failing at anything. Being kind to myself allowed me to unleash creativity.

I invite you to get curious about what your life could look like if you talked to yourself with kindness. What extraordinary accomplishment could you be capable of when you believe in your worth? You are holding my accomplishment in your hands. Now it's your turn. Your gifts are utterly and completely worthy of being shared. As Marianne Williamson says so beautifully in *A Return to Love, Reflections on the Principles of a Course in Miracles*, "Your playing small doesn't serve the world."

Consider This

Kindness begins with yourself. You are completely deserving of the same respect and love you offer to others. When you treat yourself with kindness, love yourself through the tough times, and celebrate yourself through the good times, you're creating a new tape in your mind that says "Yes, *you* are deserving of abundance in all regards despite your human imperfections." As soon as you can treat yourself with kindness it'll be that much easier for you to treat others with kindness.

For Your Journey

Write a letter of appreciation to yourself. Although this may sound daunting or silly, trust me on this: This is a very powerful exercise. Every single one of us has gifts to share. When you can appreciate your own gifts, your best self can be unleashed!

Start by closing your eyes and taking three deep breaths. Now, open to all that is magnificent about you. Tell your negative voice that he/she is not invited to this party and be gentle with yourself. What would your partner, friends, children, colleagues say are your strengths? (If you are not sure, then ask them.) Get a piece of paper and your favorite pen, sit in a quiet place that makes you feel comfortable, and start to write.

Consider
- things you've done/changes you've made;
- challenges you've overcome;
- good decisions you've made;
- lessons you've learned;
- risks you've taken;
- character traits or qualities (being kind, a good listener, protective, loyal, encouraging, optimistic).[18]

Now, address the envelope to yourself, put a stamp on it, and mail it. When it comes back to you in a couple of days and you've had some distance from the writing process, your words can be received as the gift that they are. Put the letter away in a secret place and take it out whenever you need a hug. Remember, you are a rock star!

Chapter 18

A Character Accountability Partner

---

*"Carry out a random act of kindness, with
no expectation of rewards, safe in the
knowledge that one day someone might do
the same for you."*

—Princess Diana

I MAGINE IF WE each had a *character* accountability
partner. Someone we trust and respect who helps
us to define and live the core values most precious
to us. Someone who walks alongside us reminding,
pushing, and prodding us to be the best version of
ourselves we can be. Not just someone who helps us
reach our weight loss goal or get that job promotion.
Rather a partner who helps us craft a life well lived
defined by the intangible and intrinsic character traits
of kindness, compassion, integrity, and empathy and
not by our job title, wealth, or size of our house. We
hire coaches and trainers to make us better, faster,
stronger yet we often neglect to nourish the charac-
ter traits we hope someone will use to describe us at
our funeral.

Character accountability partners will cheer us on when we lead with kindness and help us course-correct when we veer from what really matters. They will guide us to do the right thing and not just the easy thing. You don't have to win the genetic jackpot to be a person of character who leads with kindness, compassion, integrity, and empathy. All of these traits are learned behaviors and are available to each of us. Houston Kraft, founder of CharacterStrong and author of *Deep Kindness*, says, "Character is built by the 1000s of choices we make every day." When we thoughtfully choose to surround ourselves with people who reflect the characters traits most important to us, we are increasing our chances of thriving in deeply meaningful and fulfilling ways.

Our daughter Sheridan has been my *character* accountability partner. She understands and embraces my deep desire to help our world become a kinder place. She is a champion of my mission to help people everywhere know they matter. She was the first person with whom I shared my commitment to writing a book by my sixtieth birthday. I was honored and grateful when she asked if she could be my accountability partner on this milestone journey I was about to embark on.

Over the course of that year (and continuing today), she showered me with endless kind words. I knew she would be a fierce accountability partner and one who would love me through every word I wrote and every word that got stuck and couldn't seem to make it onto the page. Her appreciation for my mission of kindness and her active participation in living my mission has solidified our connection that was made the instant Dr. Druga placed her tiny newborn body on my chest thirty-one years ago.

When we know someone believes in us, the world looks so much more hospitable. Knowing we are in community with at least one person who "gets you" makes you do the happy dance. And Sheridan and I have had some epic kitchen dance parties! There's an honesty and a vulnerability that has worked its way into our relationship, and I am enriched because of it.

Sheridan would send me text messages and call me to see if I was writing and ask how it was going. She'd tell me to get going if I was wavering in my commitment. She would remind me of why I wanted to write this book and then tell me to call her after I had written a page. Most of my writing has taken place in her old bedroom at her white childhood desk overlooking our backyard. On one occasion, the day after Sheridan left from a visit, I went upstairs to write. Stuck on the window in front of the desk was a Post-it note: "I'm proud of you Mama! Keep writing... Keep believing... XOXO S." That simple note is still on the window a year later and has become my talisman. Her kind words and tough love charge my battery. I get energized by her interest and belief in me. I have a stack of precious letters from her filled with encouragement and love. She's my person and there's no combination of words yet invented to fully express my appreciation for and devotion to Sheridan.

The Man I Never Met

"Have a seat on the bed, Mom, I have a surprise for you," said Sheridan as she handed me a Kleenex. She then sat at her keyboard in the corner of the bedroom because there was no room for it in the tiny family room. I was visiting Sheridan, her then-boyfriend now-husband Colin, and Deacon, their dog, in their fifth floor apartment in Nashville overlooking Krispy Kreme on Elliston Place. Sheridan has been singing since she was a toddler in a highchair and has converted her passion for music into a career as a singer/songwriter and entrepreneur. She took a cleansing breath and told me she had written a song for me about my father, her grandfather, called "The Man I Never Met." I now understood the need for the Kleenex.

My dad was a talented piano player and singer. I've always told Sheridan she got her musical talent from him. From a young age she told me she feels a connection to her grandfather through their shared love of music that skipped me altogether. The next three minutes were frozen in time while Sheridan sang about my father and the impact he's had on her life even though they never met. The love so vibrantly and unexpectedly released through song into that bedroom uniting three generations is sealed inside my heart in that special compartment reserved for Dad. The descriptive and beautiful combination of words that Sheridan chose illustrated for me how much Dad had indeed influenced her life, even from heaven.

The lump that formed in my throat while listening to this unexpected tribute rendered me speechless. All I could do when she was finished was to gesture for another Kleenex. Sheridan used song as her vehicle to share *a few kind words* with me and she created a memory that is a treasure. I know Dad was in that room sitting on the bed with me shoulder to shoulder, his gorgeous blue eyes welling up and brimming with pride for his granddaughter.

The chorus to "The Man I Never Met":

> He has made me stronger, given me a
> sense of wonder
> that maybe I'm meant to finish what
> he started.
> So, I won't take for granted each
> God-given breath
> so I can make proud the man I never
> met.

Consider This

It's hard to become our best selves alone. We need one another. Imagine if every one of us had a *character* accountability partner cheering us on and holding our feet to the fire. The character traits of kindness, compassion, integrity and empathy are learned behaviors that are available to all of us as soon as we choose to make them a priority.

For Your Journey

Who is your *character* accountability partner in life? Surprise them with an unexpected letter of appreciation and make their day. If you don't have one, then think about someone who you admire and respect and ask them if they'd be your accountability partner. Share with them through *a few kind words* why you admire and respect them enough to ask them to jump into your life journey for a little while. They will be honored. Or offer to be a *character* accountability partner for someone else. We need each other!

Chapter 19

Serendipity

"When somebody receives a letter, it's a moment of serendipity. Even your own anticipation of your letter arriving in the mail for your recipient will boost your happiness."

—Jackie Martin

S ERENDIPITY IS ONE of my most favorite words. I can't say it or think about it and not smile. Maybe it's because I associate it with the scrumptious, slurpable, sharing-size hot chocolate the restaurant Serendipity in New York City is famous for, or because it's the title of one of my most favorite happily-ever-after romantic comedies.

The definition of serendipity is "the phenomenon of finding valuable or agreeable things not sought for." That's exactly the delicious feeling the recipient and the writer get to experience when an unexpected letter of appreciation is released into the world. It's like the universe aligning at just the right time to give you exactly what you need when you didn't even know you needed it.

Two days after my mother passed away, I was scheduled to share my workshop at a coffee hosted by my dear friend Laura. She had twenty friends coming to her beautiful home to hear my story of *A Few Kind Words* and be in fellowship with one another. This was four days before Mom's funeral, fifteen days after I had written my final letter in my yearlong challenge, and three weeks before the Covid lockdown that would turn our world upside down. Although Laura graciously asked me if I wanted to cancel my talk, I had total clarity that I wanted/needed to share my story with this group of friends on our scheduled day.

I arrived home from Long Island, where I'd been with my mother in her final hours, late the night before my workshop. I remember unloading the car with Tom and filling our living room with some remnants of my mother's life: a dropleaf dining room table, a painting of our golden retriever Cuddles, and a small chest of drawers filled with old Christmas cards from friends near and far she couldn't throw away. I woke up the next morning, reviewed my presentation, and walked into the waiting arms of my friend. Just like a hug from my mother would elicit tears, I was afraid feeling Laura's loving support would send me into an emotional spiral. Instead, I felt bolstered by her friendship and grateful for the opportunity to be surrounded by a community of old and new friends who lifted me up and held me in the gentlest and kindest way. The workshop gave me an opportunity to talk about my parents, now reunited after thirty-three years, and for that I am eternally grateful.

I always close my workshop with a challenge to write a letter of appreciation to someone special and offer the suggestion that if it feels a bit overwhelming to write to someone close to you, then start with someone you admire and respect but are not that close to. Jess, one of the attendees, did just that and got to feel the nourishing power of connection firsthand. If I had canceled the workshop, maybe Jess and Mrs. Pervin, her third and fourth grade teacher, never would have had their serendipitous reunion.

Jess and the Teacher Who Changed Her Life

When Jess was in third grade in the Princeton public school, her teacher, Mrs. Pervin, changed her life. She was the first person to believe in the gifts Jess possessed, and that made Jess begin to believe in herself. Jess struggled with reading, writing, and spelling until Mrs. Pervin came into her life. With patience, care, and the conviction that everyone can conquer the world, Jess's teacher encouraged her and gave her the gift of confidence.

Is there a greater gift you can give to a child? It was a joyful day when Jess learned that Mrs. Pervin was also moving up to the fourth grade the following year and she'd be her teacher once again. What Jess remembers most about those two years are the unwavering support of a nurturing and kind teacher, and Celia, the new and incredibly creative girl who moved from Colorado for just those two years and became her best friend. When you're an eight-year-old girl, your best friend is your universe, and when you have a teacher who "gets you," lasting memories are made.

After fourth grade, Celia moved back to Colorado and Jess left Mrs. Pervin's safe and comfortable classroom, but both people remained imprinted on her heart. Jess lost touch with her best friend until Facebook reconnected them a few years ago. The wonderful connection they felt on the first day of third grade in September 1978 was still there. Within just a few DMs they were reminiscing about Mrs. Pervin and sharing old photos of elementary school days. Celia even found an old story from fourth grade on which Mrs. Pervin had written: "You have a gift with words and one day you are going to write a book!" What Jess learned about her rediscovered friend is that she is a celebrated chef in London and has written numerous vegetarian cookbooks. Mrs. Pervin believed in Celia too!

After Jess left my workshop on that February day in 2020, she knew that Mrs. Pervin would be her letter recipient. Jess gathered her thoughts, found some stationery, and wrote a heartfelt, unexpected letter of appreciation to the teacher who changed her life nearly four decades earlier. She told her how she and Celia had recently reconnected and that much of their conversations centered around what an inspiration

Mrs. Pervin was to both girls, one who struggled with writing and reading and the other who was new to town.

Jess enclosed a copy of Celia's most recent cookbook, *SuperVeg*, with her letter and then began to search for an address for this special woman. Her first call was to the Princeton Public School administration office, but they weren't able to supply any information about retired teachers. Next, she went to Google and, through whitepages.com, found her favorite teacher still living in Princeton only a few miles from where Jess lives with her husband Rich and their three kids. Jess drove to her home to hand deliver her letter and Celia's book, but Mrs. Pervin wasn't home. She left the package.

Not long after, she received a phone call from a teary Mrs. Pervin telling Jess how lovely her letter was and that no one had ever done something quite like that for her before. Their reconnection was as joyful as Jess had imagined it could be. At eighty-one years old, Mrs. Pervin still made Jess feel special, and Jess in turn helped Mrs. Pervin feel valued, important, and perhaps helped validate all those years of hard work as a teacher. They talked for a while, reminiscing, re-awakening a dormant relationship, letting each other know that they matter. After their phone call Jess relayed the story to Celia and then Celia and Mrs. Pervin also had their own beautiful reconnection, all facilitated by a letter of appreciation. Together this trio felt energized and uplifted because

Jess took the time to share *a few kind words*. The ripple effects were felt all the way to London where Celia still lives.

Consider This

The definition of serendipity is "the phenomenon of finding valuable or agreeable things not sought for." That's exactly the nourishing feeling that the recipient and the writer get to experience when an unexpected letter of appreciation is released into the world. It's like the universe aligning at just the right time to give you exactly what you need when you didn't even know you needed it.

For Your Journey

Do you have a favorite teacher or mentor from your childhood who has left an imprint on your heart or influenced the best parts of who you are today? Please write to them. It's never too late to share your appreciation. If that special person has passed on, consider tracking down a family member of your mentor and sharing your kind memories with them. So many good feelings would be released.

Chapter 20

It's Liberating to Grow Into a Better Person

"Go and love someone exactly as they are. And then watch how quickly they transform into the greatest, truest version of themselves. When one feels seen and appreciated in their own essence, one is instantly empowered."

—Wes Angelozzi

I T's LIBERATING TO keep growing into a better version of yourself. When I led with kindness, I became someone I liked more. When I was able to clear the clutter from my mind and make kindness a habit, I realized that kindness is my core value.

The definition of values is "a set of beliefs or opinions that influence how you live your life." I didn't set out to uncover my core value when I started this challenge; it was just one of the defining benefits that emerged. Kindness, through *A Few Kind Words*, allows me to feel more connected, and when I feel more connected, I treat myself and others better. I like that.

I've come to learn that when we lead our lives with our core value as our beacon, choices become easier, life becomes clearer, and elusive happiness isn't so elusive anymore. What value is non-negotiable to you? When you can answer that question, consider filtering decisions both big and small through that value filter and see if life becomes a little clearer.

Questions to Help Define
Your Personal Core Values

Spend time in personal reflection writing about what moves you. The following are questions to help start this exploration. Your responses are clues you can use to identify your core value system.

- Who do you admire and why? Think of some positive role models who inspire you to live a meaningful life.
- What inspires you to take action? Often our core values reveal themselves through our actions. Can you think of a situation when you took a stand for someone or something?
- When do you feel most like yourself? When you're in situations that allow you to be authentic, that's a clue that you are in alignment with your values.[19]

I became a better caregiver and advocate for my mother when I filtered hundreds of decisions through my kindness filter. My mother's slow decline happened over the course of my year of letter writing challenge—and, in some ways, the letters saved me. My letters helped lift me up when I was spiraling downward. They forced me to find light in the ever-growing dimness that was encircling Mom, Wendy, and me. Had I not been engaged in the mindful practice of writing these letters during that time, I would've missed out on countless precious gems of connection and community around Mom's care. I possibly would've missed the dignity in Mom's decline.

Building Collaboration

One day, I was driving across the Verrazano Bridge, heading to Long Island to meet Wendy for a postponed (due to Covid) Christmas lunch. It was a bluebird day. As I looked to my left at the New York City skyline and then to my right at the sparkling ocean whose vast horizon called to me, I realized I felt relaxed and hopeful. It dawned on me that this was the first time in forever that I'd felt that way while crossing the bridge heading to my hometown in Long Island.

For a year and a half, at least once a week, I had made the round-trip congested drive from Pennington, New Jersey, to Roslyn, New York, to care for our declining mother. But it wasn't the traffic that caused me the most angst; it was worrying about how my time with my mother would be. She had been a feisty real estate agent until she was over 88 years of age. When she was eighty-seven, she sold thirteen co-ops in the community where she lived and earned the nickname "The Co-op Queen." This gave her purpose. Soon after retiring it was like her body decided to retire, too. Over the course of the next four and a half years, Mom overcame melanoma, colon cancer, lymphoma, and a broken hip. It was the beginning of a long and challenging time. Mom had lovingly cared for us for decades and now it was our turn to care for her. Our independent, courageous, and capable mother hated living in her CCRC, but she rarely complained. Guilt is a wasted emotion, as we have all heard, but wow it is a powerful one.

It was a few months after Mom broke her hip that I decided to go on my yearlong letter writing journey. I do believe when we're open to it, the universe gives us what we need. This practice helped yank me out of my inward wallowing and forced me to focus outward. I became more open to noticing people around me. It helped me listen more intently, practice patience, and ask about the lives of those who were now, unexpectedly, in my life. Every time I connected with someone in Mom's community, I felt a little bit of stress drain away. The *A Few Kind Words* journey helped me recognize each one of the caregivers had a life beyond my mother's walls. They were people, too, with their own stresses and worries. Each person who we relied on for Mom's care softened when they received my letter. More importantly, I softened to each one of them when I looked for and found what made them special. What a waste it would have been if I only remembered the fear and the stress.

The following is a sampling of the letter recipients I wrote to from Mom's CCRC:

- Renee, the social worker and our lifeline. Her compassion, listening skills, and level of caring for our family made our experience bearable. While we were Mom's advocate, she was Wendy's and my advocate.

- Kevin, the front desk manager, made me feel like he was genuinely happy to see me every time I arrived after my long car trip. He eased my transition from getting there to being here.

- Varsha, the nurse who wore a cloak of calm and caring that instantly was transferred to me.

- Bernadette, another resident's personal aide, who scooped Mom up and made sure that she was always included and was our eyes when we weren't there.

- Sylvia, Mom's assisted living aide, took extra time with Mom and exhibited a degree of patience that was often lacking in other aides.

- Julie, our aide who treated Mom with the most loving and respectful care. If Julie wasn't an angel in her prior life, she will be in her next.

- Xio, Mom's dining room server whose smile melted our angst and warmed our hearts.

Every letter I wrote during Mom's last year was a gift to myself. I felt calmer and more open to collaboration each time I took a moment to share my appreciation. I hope you will also consider taking the time to slow down and notice those around you who you need to collaborate with in your personal and professional life. Writing these letters was medicine for my soul and helped me get through one of the most difficult times in my life. It reminded me that it takes a village, and we all need each other. When we share appreciations, the world sparkles a bit more, just like the ocean was doing under the clear blue sky and bright sun as I drove over the Verrazano Bridge.

Consider This

I became a better person when I chose to lead my life with my core value—kindness. I've come to learn that when we lead our lives with our core value as our beacon, choices become easier, life becomes clearer, and elusive happiness isn't so elusive anymore. It helped me be open to collaboration with my mother's caregivers and provided a way for me to feel like I was part of a community and not so alone. Everything is possible when you don't feel alone. What value is non-negotiable to you?

For Your Journey

Think about who you need to collaborate with and write them a letter of appreciation. If this feels hard then even more reason to stick with it and try it. True collaboration only works if you approach it with a positive attitude. First, invest some time in getting to know your collaboration partner by listening and asking questions. Be open to finding their attributes. Everyone has them; you just may have to look a little harder for some. Then, share your appreciation. Like magic, watch yourself soften into a more rewarding, productive, and impactful collaboration.

Chapter 21

What We DO Matters

"I got your beautiful note... I am going to laminate it."

—Debbie, letter recipient

M Y FRIEND RICHARD loves peonies as much as I do. He has a beautiful garden with an abundance of these magnificent showstoppers.

The first year of the pandemic, when the world was shut down including florists, Richard's big heart prompted him to share his abundance with his neighbors. He set up a little stand on the curb in front of his home with one kind word written on the bucket, *FREE*. He filled the bucket with cut stems of peonies and hoped that his simple offering could bring some unexpected joy into the lives of his neighbors during this time of isolation.

He and his partner happened to be looking out the window when the FedEx driver came by. She passed the house and stopped the truck. She got out of her truck and walked back to the bucket, selected

a stem and actually skipped back to her truck. I don't
know if it was the delight of a free peony or the sim-
ple act of generosity that made her skip, but when
was the last time you saw an adult skip from pure
un"adult"erated joy? She then wrote a thank you note
on a FedEx label and left it at their door.

A neighbor whom they had never met was so
touched by Richard's act that she introduced her-
self in order to offer her thanks. A strong friendship
has since developed. Richard received many notes of
appreciation for his act of kindness. What we choose
to DO, does indeed matter!

While my mission is to let people everywhere
know *they* matter, that means what I *do* matters first.
What we do is a reflection of who we are. It's our
value system on display. It's about taking action.
I have to actually tell my recipient what I appreci-
ate about them. Otherwise, it's just a kind thought
that doesn't count. I have to make room in my life
for appreciations to show up. What can each one of
us do that can make someone "skip" like the FedEx
driver? When we make the proactive choice to be
involved with something bigger than ourselves, that's
when the life satisfaction scale starts to tip away from
"fine" towards exhilarating. Maria Shriver, in her
Sunday Paper says, "None of us are too small to make
an impact on someone's life. None of us are too small
to leave an imprint on someone's heart. It's why we
are here."[20]

Hope Isn't Canceled

Five weeks after I'd written my last letter in my challenge, the world shut down because of an unimaginable pandemic. The mandate to stay home was scary and, at the beginning, a welcomed gift for me with no children at home. All day in yoga clothes, time to clean out closets and binge watch shows on our to-watch list. Bra and hair washing optional.

For others, it was a living hell. Our teacher friends had to take a crash course in technology and learn how to teach online in a matter of two weeks, shifting the way teachers have taught and children have learned for generations: in person and hands on. For parents with children at home, the impossible was being asked of them with no advance warning: Help the kids learn online while both parents work from home and manage everyone's emotional needs with no social outlets allowed.

Endless questions with no clear answers. Do we wipe down all the groceries and leave them in the garage overnight or not? Can we take a walk with our friends if we stay on opposite sides of the road? Can we visit our ninety-year-old mother-in-law who lives alone? Countless people lost their jobs overnight in almost every industry. Living in isolation from our extended families, friends, and neighbors was a novelty for maybe a week but grew to be intolerable over the course of weeks and months. We thrive on community and connection. I felt compelled to share *a few kind words* with our community and give people an opportunity to connect in a safe and uplifting way.

My brother-in-law donated the full sheet of plywood he had stored in his garage, and I painted it white. In large blue print I wrote HOPE ISN'T CANCELED across the board and added a small piece of wood with the request to "add your own messages of hope." Tom screwed the small sign to the big sign, and we added a cup holder with markers. We strapped it to the roof of our car and drove it to the entrance of our neighborhood. We attached it to the metal railings overlooking a small brook and waited across the street. Within a few minutes the first person walked by. We watched her read the sign and then grab a marker and add her own message: "Resilience." I rode my bike back to the sign about four hours later and found there were now six messages, including one clearly written in a young child's handwriting saying "treat others how you want to be treated." The next day there were fifteen, and within a week there was barely any room to write. The sign of hope was doing what I'd hoped, providing a channel for us to feel connected and supported and serving as a reminder that "we will get through this together," as an early writer wrote.

We need one another, and our words spoken and written became our beacon of hope during this remarkable time of fear. Everything looks a little less scary when we can talk about it with one another or read universal messages of hope or listen to an entire neighborhood in Italy sing in unison out of their windows at 6 p.m. every night. When we can each carry a little piece of the fear of the unknown, then the weight becomes more evenly distributed and bearable.

To ease each other's burden. Isn't that our job as human*kind*?

I've no idea how many lives were touched by my sign of hope. I left it up for four months and thousands of cars and walkers and bikers passed by it. A friend with a graduating senior shared a video that the high school administration sent to each graduating family, and my sign was at the end of the video. There was a photo of it in a local newspaper with words of encouragement. My friend's second grade daughter included a photo of it in a homework assignment. This pandemic reinforced for me, and I believe it probably did for you, too, that when we're stripped bare of our livelihoods and our luxuries our words and our relationships are really all we have.

Consider This

What we do matters! What we do is a reflection of who we are. It's our value system on display. It's about making the choice to take action that makes our world a more humane place. In an uncertain world, connection is more important than ever. Our words and our actions have a lasting impact.

For Your Journey

How can you spread *a few kind words* in your community and encourage connection and a shared purpose? Considering starting a "Just Because" campaign......

- Have a "Make Someone's Day" stand where you offer notecards and pens for people to share a kind thought about someone that they can then deliver to their someone special.
- Have a lemonade stand and offer the lemonade for *free*.
- Offer to mow your neighbor's lawn or weed their garden.
- Double your dinner recipe and deliver a surprise meal to someone.
- Share the bounty from your garden

...Just because!

Chapter 22

People Who Have Passed

"I don't think that I have ever been given a gift like the one you gave me. I cherish your letter. It meant more to me than you know. Thank you for such a beautiful gift. I read it often."

—Alesia, letter recipient

SOMETIMES OUR FAVORITE, most beloved people— those who have loved us into being—leave us before we get the chance to share *a few kind words*. Sometimes, we had the chance but weren't ready to share. Sometimes fear of getting vulnerable held us back. Sometimes, we have regrets about what was never shared, and sometimes, we feel compelled to say what we did say one more time.

It's never too late to share *a few kind words* with the person who has gone before you.

It's healing, soothing, and nourishing to tell your beloved why you miss them and how they made a lasting impression on your life. It's my belief that although this person may not be able to hold your hand physically, they can fill your heart spiritually as they receive your words of affirmation.

When I wrote my last letter to Dad, thirty-three years and nine days after he passed away, I could feel his energy in the room. When I read the letter out loud to him, I received a response that will forever live in the space in my heart reserved just for him, until we meet again. Here's my story and why I know that writing unexpected letters of appreciation to people who've passed is just as empowering, energizing, and uplifting as writing to people who are still here. It's never too late to further connections. Who's filling your heart right now?

A Wind Hug

I was standing on top of the knoll between the lake and the reservoir behind our house. The grass was brown and trampled down after the last snowfall had melted a few days before. The bare tree branches formed a mosaic around the lake. The geese had flown south but there were still two pure white swans at the far end of the lake. I never could understand why they stayed all winter, but they'd become my friends.

We're lucky to have acres of conservation land behind our home. I walk back there most days with our dog, Ella, and often Tom and any friends who want to join. It's my happy place. I love the change of scenery in this special 1.5-mile loop we feel blessed to call our backyard. First there's the narrow trail through woods where you have to dodge the prickly, invasive rose branches that keep reaching out in greeting. The path then opens into a field the farmer alternately plants with soy, winter wheat, or allows to go fallow.

Next is the peaceful lake followed by a long meandering trail through the woods that allows glimpses of Stony Brook which companionably flows nearby, at one spot offering a swimming hole for the dogs. The woods are littered with crisscrossed trees that have fallen during countless storms over the twenty-three years we've been walking these trails, offering seats for reflection. It was on one of these fallen trees that I had planned to sit and read out loud my letter to Dad, finally offering him *a few kind words*.

It was February 9, 2020, the last day of my self-imposed, yearlong letter writing challenge. As I knew on the plane that day when the idea for this challenge came to me, my last letter would be to my father, Buzz Willis. I was anxious as this day approached, not sure what it would feel like to write a letter to someone who'd passed away so long ago. Someone who was so important to me, who I had lost when I was a newly engaged young adult and now, I was a grandmother.

I sat at the kitchen counter with a notecard, pen in hand and a box of Kleenex by my side. I closed my eyes for quite a while and filled my being with images and memories of Dad and then I wrote. It was surprisingly joyful to feel like I was connecting with Dad on a deeper level than I had in a long time. Although I've never doubted that Dad knew I loved him, it was important for me to offer him what he'd asked for from everyone in his family: *a few kind words*. I finished the letter, sealed it with a kiss before putting it in the envelope, and held it against my heart. I put on my down jacket and boots, grabbed my gloves, and headed for the woods to read my letter to Dad.

The day was magnificently beautiful. The sky was the color of my favorite and elusive bluebirds. Not a cloud to be seen. It was cold but the sun made me feel invigorated rather than chilled. I passed through the narrow trail and reached my face toward the sun as I walked on the worn path through the field. When I got to the knoll by the lake, I suddenly felt compelled to stop. I was filled with the conviction to read the letter to Dad there and not sitting on the fallen log in the woods where I had envisioned reading it.

The lake was calling to me. There wasn't a breath of wind. As I gazed over the lake it was like looking at a painting. The water was perfect glass and there was no movement. The stillness gave me the impression the lake was holding its breath waiting to receive my words. I looked around and hoped no one was coming because they would see a crazy lady reading a letter aloud to no one. I took a deep breath and read my letter to Dad.

The very instant I finished reading, the most incredible thing happened. An enormous swirling wind came out of nowhere and wrapped itself around me over and over again. The wind was so strong I had to take a step back to catch my balance. My hair blew into my face, and I had to grasp the letter tightly before it blew away. And then it stopped. The still-ness took over again. Although I had always heard of a swirling wind, I'd never taken a second to imagine what that feels like. Well now I know. It felt like the most precious, miraculous hug from Dad.

I had spent a lot of time thinking about the writing and the reading of this long overdue letter, but I hadn't spent any time thinking about receiving a sign from Dad. That sudden, strong wind that was circling me again and again was a beloved bearhug from Dad. With every part of my being, I know that Dad received my *few kind words* and I received back a connection I never dreamed possible.

My letter to Dad:

———

Dear Dad,   *2-9-2020*

Better late than never… All you ever said you wanted for your birthday or Christmas was "a few kind words." None of us in the family knew how to give that to you at the time. You left us far too early and decades before I figured out that words were the gift that you cherished. Now, 33 years and 9 days later, I offer you the gift of a few kind words.

Dad, you dazzled me as a child and a young woman. Your beautiful blue eyes danced with love and joy when you smiled. Your enormous bear hugs solved all the problems of the world and sustained me on the best and worst days. A laughing attack

———

with you still stands as one of my favorite activities of all time. I am smiling at the memory of being a little irreverent together when Mom wasn't looking. You were such an elegant dancer, and I can still hear you saying, "When I was young, dancing was a contact sport." You defined for me what grace looked like. You simply never shared a harsh word, judgement, or criticism—ever. What a rare and precious trait you role-modeled for me. You were gentle and kind, treating people with respect—always. Dad, you matter, and you have always mattered! I am so sorry that I didn't take the time to say that when you were alive. You guide me every day. Your gentle, loving spirit is an elixir for my soul.

Dad, you're still teaching me valuable lessons three decades later guiding me to understand, embrace, and share the energizing power of A Few Kind Words. This yearlong letter writing journey has made me realize that we're more alike than I ever thought. Words of affirmation are indeed the most cherished gift that we give and receive. This journey has brought a calm and joy into my life that was unexpected and life changing. I am telling the world your story and hoping to inspire a movement of kindness through writing unexpected letters of kindness. You were brave enough to ask for what you wanted all those years ago and now it's my greatest privilege to partner with you on this inspiring journey. I hope that I can make you proud. I think the greatest gift for me this year is that you've come alive for me again in the most beautiful way. I feel a connection to you that while not lost, was diminished for a few decades.

Dad, your bright light is still shining and through me you are lighting the way for the world to enjoy the simple and powerful gift of kindness. I miss you every day, but I know that you're walking with me. I want more than anything to be sharing a black and white milkshake with you right now talking about anything and nothing. Instead, I promise you Dad that for the rest of my life I will help people everywhere understand your gift of a few kind words. I love you with all of my being. With gratitude and appreciation,

Forever your little girl, Tracey

Consider This

Our loved ones are always with us. It's never too late to share *a few kind words* with anyone who holds a place in your heart. Maybe you'll not receive a wind hug, but spending quality time communing with an important person in your life is always meaningful.

For Your Journey

Who in your life has passed that is filling your heart and mind? Consider writing them a letter. You can read it out loud to just yourself or read it to someone else who loved that person or loves you, or just write the letter, seal it with a kiss, and remember.

My dad, Buzz Willis

Chapter 23

Have You Decided What KIND of Person You'd Like to Be?

---

*"Focusing on the good balances out the
negative and reminds us of who we are. I
reflected on what happens to one's body
when kindness has been bestowed upon it.
It calms down. It settles. It relaxes and lets
down its guard. When one opens themselves
to acts of kindness, life feels more hopeful,
positive, and humanistic. It's that simple."*

—Maria Shriver

THE LAST TIME I saw Dad was December 30, 1986,
when Tom and I celebrated our engagement
with both sets of parents at Fuddruckers Restaurant
in New Jersey halfway between their homes. We
toasted our bright future and the joining together of
our families. It was a happy evening filled with love.

I can remember the feel of Dad's bear hug and his
whispered, "Love you, sweetheart, see you in a few
weeks," as we said goodbye.

Our family Christmas present that year was

tickets to a Broadway musical in late January. A huge snowstorm hit the East Coast the day of our show and made travel impossible from Boston to New York City for me, and even from Long Island to the City for my parents. I can't remember what Broadway show we were supposed to see, but I do know that snowstorm robbed me of the last opportunity to spend quality time with one of my most favorite people in the world, my dad. Nine days later he was gone.

But here it is, three and a half decades later, and although Dad and I missed out on attending that one last musical, his refrain of *a few kind words* has brought us together for a ride of a lifetime. He is my constant companion on this journey that has improved the quality of my life and I hope has opened you up to your own beautiful possibilities.

We've got this. You've got this! We all have kind thoughts. That's the easy part. All you have to do is transfer those lovely thoughts to words that are written or spoken. When they are released and shared, they explode with brilliance, like the finale of your favorite Fourth of July fireworks display. They dance in the light of acknowledgment as they are absorbed by your recipient. Who knows, maybe your recipient will be encouraged to pass on the light, and so it goes. We can all be part of the change we want to see in this magnificent world we share. We just need to make the proactive choice to do it. It takes courage and commitment to stand in the power of kindness, but when we make it a priority, we can all be part of that change, one letter or action at a time.

We can never know what it really feels like to walk in someone else's shoes, but we do know that intentional kindness feels good every single time it's offered and every single time it's received. So let's assume that every person you come in contact with could use a boost. As often as you can, offer them the boost of *a few kind words* and be part of something bigger than yourself. Something expansive and beautiful.

A Few KindWords has given me a meaningful coping strategy to help navigate all that fractures our world today and has reacquainted me with what really matters most, our relationships. I hope you feel inspired to share your kind thoughts often and experience for yourself the emotional and physical abundance that accompanies this positivity practice. There's so much to be appreciated in all the people who surround us on a daily basis.

Look up, engage, listen, linger, and then share what you observe and what you feel. Talk about kindness around the dinner table. Bring the discussion to your schools, your workplaces, and your neighborhoods. Look for opportunities to broaden your circle of love. It's what we're here to do. It's what we need to do.

Go ahead.....Make Someone's Day!

Conclusion

Join the A Few Kind Words Global Movement

WOULDN'T IT BE amazing if people all over the world were opening their mailboxes and finding unexpected handwritten letters of appreciation? Just imagine the feel-good energy that would be released into the universe...

Let's make kindness go viral!

The mission is bold, but the idea is simple... It's time to help people everywhere know they matter! Can we go around the world? Start with someone in your household or hometown. Then reach farther.

How To Do This

1. Who's the first person who comes to your mind? Don't pause. Write them an unexpected letter of appreciation, then mail it or deliver it.

2. Scan the QR code below or go to my website *afewkindwords.net* and under the "Share Your Stories" tab fill out the form with how many letters you have written and *please*, share your stories of connection with me so I can then share them with my audience. We all want to be uplifted by your stories. Kindness is contagious.

3. Follow me on my social media sites and share with your family & friends!
Instagram: @afewkindwordschallenge
Facebook Group: @AFewKindWordsCommunity

Bonus: This QR code will also take you to hear the song written about my father "The Man I Never Met," by our daughter, Sheridan Gates

I can't wait to get to know you and hear how kindness has positively impacted your life. Welcome to the *A Few KindWords* community, I'm so glad you're here!

Endnotes

[1] Dr. Robert Waldinger and Dr. Marc Schulz, *The Good Life: Lessons from the World's Longest Scientific Study of Happiness* (New York: Simon & Schuster, 2023).

[2] Houston Kraft, "Nice vs Kind: Short." Vimeo, January 30, 2020, vimeo.com/388314995/e49971338e.

[3] S.M. Toepfer, K. Cichy, and P. Peters, "Letters of Gratitude: Further Evidence for Author Benefits," *Journal of Happiness Studies* 13, 187-201 (2012).

[4] Dr. Mark Hyman, "Creating Healthier Relationships," undated blog post, at drhyman.com/blog.

[5] Team Brook, "The Unexpected Benefits of Letting Writing," blog post, May 7, 2020, at marthabrook.com.

[6] S.M. Toepfer, K. Cichy, and P. Peters, "Letters of Gratitude: Further Evidence for Author Benefits," *Journal of Happiness Studies* 13, 187-201 (2012).

[7] "Millennials can be surprisingly old fashioned with communication, study finds," SWNS Digital, September 6, 2021, at swnsdigital.com.

[8] Amit Kumar and Nicholas Epley, "Undervaluing gratitude: Expressers misunderstand the consequences of showing appreciation," *Psychological Science* 29, no. 9 (2018): 1423-35.

[9] Lisa Currie, "Why teaching kindness in schools is essential to reduce bullying," Edutopia.org, blog post, August 10, 2015.

[10] Inspired Kindness Team, "Make kindness louder than hate," undated blog post, Inspirekindness.com.

[11] Mental Health Foundation, "Kindness and Mental Health," updated web page reflecting on a 2020 study in the UK, at mentalhealth.org.uk.

[12] Happiness.com, "The Power of Kindness: The ripple effect of being nice," undated web page at Happiness.com.

[13] Leah Collins, "Job Unhappiness Is at a Staggering All-Time High, According to Gallup." CNBC, August 12, 2022, at CNBC.com.

[14] Lynne Levy, "5 Reasons Kindness Matters." Workhuman.com. November 13, 2020, at Workhuman.com/resources.

[15] Simon Sinek, *Start with Why: How Great Leaders Inspire Everyone to Take Action* (New York: Portfolio, 2009).

[16] Quoted by Meghan Rabbitt in "Do You Want to Expand Your Capacity to Love Others and Yourself?" The Sunday Paper, January 28, 2023, at MariaShriver.com.

[17] Stacey Lindsay, "Fierce Intimacy Is Where It's At: Wondering If You Have It—Or How to Get It? Read On," September 6, 2016, at Mariashriver.com.

[18] Adapted from Katie Keridan, "How to Write a Mindful Thankful Letter," Breathe Together Yoga. April 22, 2021, at Breathetogetheryoga.com.

[19] "Defining Your List of Values and Beliefs (with 102 examples)," SoulSALT, January 29, 2022, web page at Soulsalt.com.

[20] Maria Shriver, "The Power of Inclusion." *The Sunday Paper*, June 24, 2023.

Acknowledgments

I have endless gratitude for the community of kindness ambassadors who believe in my mission and gave of their time and talent to help make my dream of writing a book a reality. My circle of love continues to grow exponentially because of all of you.

With deep appreciation for:

My husband Tom Gates, who has been a champion of my message and mission from the start, I love you completely. Your belief in me and support sustains me and lifts me up every day.

Our daughter, Sheridan Gates Montemarano, for being my accountability partner, my on- call technical support, and my daily sounding board. Your patience, your thoughtful input and your loving care enriched this journey for me.

Our son Ren Gates, for your unwavering enthusiasm for my project and gentle encouragement.

Dianne Tappe, for your wise counsel and utter and complete conviction that this book needed to be written. Your enthusiasm for and deep interest in every aspect of this book project touched me to the core, energized me and helped me across the finish line.

My early readers: for providing valuable insight, suggestions, and affirmations that helped me share my message in the best possible light. Each one of you willingly gave of your precious time to read my early drafts and I will always be grateful to you for your interest, support and friendship: Sharon Altmeyer, Callie Cote, Terri Epstein, Susan Finlay, Ren Gates, Tom Gates, Mark McLaughlin, Sheridan Montemarano, Hugh O'Neill, Barb Phelan, Michael Pottinger, Debbie Schlette, Molly Schneider, and Dianne Tappe.

Alexandra Deubner, my life coach, for helping me realize I did have a book inside of me just waiting to be written. That "bed jumping" joy is sealed in my heart.

Louise Wellemeyer, for the candles I lit every day when I sat down to write and for your unbridled excitement and support.

My parents, Janet and Buzz Willis, for loving me.

Corrine Casanova for her thoughtful developmental edit that helped to craft the format of the book and Meredith Tennant, for her line edit.

The team at Epigraph Publishing Services for your thoughtful guidance in bringing my book to life.

The extensive community of appreciators who are all around us willing to lead with kindness and do their part to make this world a kinder place. You inspire me. My heart is full.

Printed in the USA
CPSIA information can be obtained
at www.ICGtesting.com
LVHW082036041123
762998LV00035B/1193/J